Heartful Leadership

A Primer for Transforming Education

Dr. Wolfgang Amann

Dr. Pankaj Gupta

Dr. Shiv Tripathi

wp **walnutpublication**
.com

INDIA • UK • USA

Paperback ISBN: 978-1-957302-00-3

Hardback ISBN: 978-1-957302-01-0

eBook ISBN: 978-1-957302-02-7

First Published in January 2022

Published by Walnut Publication

(an imprint of Vyusta Ventures LLP)

www.walnutpublication.com

USA

6834 Cantrell Road #2096, Little Rock, AR 72207, USA

India

#625, Esplanade One, Rasulgarh, Bhubaneswar – 751010, India
#55 S/F, Panchkuian Marg, Connaught Place, New Delhi - 110001, India

UK

International House, 12 Constance Street, London E16 2DQ, United Kingdom

Contents

List of Figures

List of Tables

Foreword

COVID-19 started to challenge established solutions in education from in early 2020. Many institutions were clearly behind when it comes to modern forms and delivery format of learning. Leaders of these institutions practically had not choice other than rethinking their set-ups. The much-needed change does refer to technology, but not only. At times an entire school year was lost, and psychologists predict lasting damage of limited home-schooling and a lack of socialization opportunities. Yet, Winston Churchill once said "never let a good crisis go to waste". Therefore, we put together this book at the right time. As COVID-19 questioned established solutions in education and as the wind of change is blowing strongly, we hope that institutional leaders and policymakers in the educational sector perceive current times as an opportunity for holistic change. Not only technologies for delivery ought to adapt but also the humanism we foster in education. It shows in the degree to which we value and enhance human dignity, in the way we promote heartfulness both amongst institutional leaders as well as of parts of educational ideals and curricula. In the age of COVID-19 and the rise of AI, we ought to carefully prepare a system-wide change in education to ready our societies as well as graduates for the challenges ahead. If we use this current crisis, we can emerge better prepared, more resilient, and more focused on what really matters. Alternatively, we can perpetuate a dated system for long gone times. The choice is up to us. We hope the reader will find inspiration in this book on why to change as well as how. The book can best be understood as a buffet of ideas. Read selectively about what excites you the most and ideally conceive change that actually impacts practices.

Chapter 1: Heartful leadership for transforming education and driving humanism and sustainability

Wolfgang Amann, Shiv Tripathi and Pankaj Gupta

1.1. Why transformational education needs heartfulness

Education leaders today have great responsibility to drive the changes across the entire education value-chain while contributing to accomplishing the sustainable development goals (SDGs) directly through SDG4 (Quality Education). In context of higher education, the responsibility is even more due to its role in capacity building for successful lives. Higher education is also considered important for knowledge creation and capacity building to support realization of rest of the SDGs.

The education links not only caters to training and skill building but should also prepare individuals to serve the purpose of humanity, however, the question remains regarding what kind of education systems are required to contribute towards purpose of humanity. Across the globe, we have seen rising number of institutions with focus on preparing the human capital for industry and organizations and thus, converting the education as a means to achieve certain tangible and material ends. The goal of education for a creative society cannot be economic, it must be cultural, and it must be to enhance multi-fold and not just sustain culture.

Looking at how largely the education systems are getting geared to in response to the changes in the industries in the current era we realize that it is training students on a mass scale in all emerging knowledge areas (for example, latest technologies and applications), which are utilized to serve narrow commercial interests rather broader human goals. The design principle of tuning of education systems to demands of the industry is the fundamental flaw in education system design in the current era. We, as an academic institution, must answer how can we as human society progress to achieve the aesthetic and creative potential of every individual? Rather than being entrenched in the shackles of survival how can we as individuals and society support each other to reach our creative potentials?

In order to align the education for sustainability, the purpose and vision of educational institutions must be transformed. What needs to be thought of with regards to the desired higher education system for driving sustainability involves consideration of issues relating to academic course contents, pedagogy as well as the supporting institutional environment and vision.

Considering the extinction of several languages, dialects, art forms, cultural traditions, dance forms etc., all but expressions of human creativity, human civilization is heading towards a possible homogenization. Is education serving the right ends? Can this type of education system help in contributing towards the desired sustainability path? This is the right juncture to pose these very pertinent and important questions. If largely the direction of education is wrong are there not silver bullets? The emerging liberal arts education may have some answers! But the question remains, how?

1.2. How heartful leadership supports transformational education

While aiming for the desired transformation in our education system, we can learn from the good practices from the different educational traditions. For example, the ancient Indian education system of 'Gurukul', which used to be disjunct from the world of practice i.e., business, politics, and society, offers a great model of education for larger human development goals. Further, a liberal arts educational curriculum was a typical of the ancient Gurukul system wherein the gurus used to educate the pupils through various pedagogies a variety of subjects which helped them make sense of the world and act in future based on the holistic knowledge acquired. Values such as equality of self-vision and unity were deeply ingrained in the pupils through their living practices at the Gurukul. This ensured creation of a free individual who was able to live a life for the society and not for self-interest. The ancient wisdom on education was able to define the purpose of education beyond narrow self-interested ends to pursuit of aesthetics i.e. expression of creativity and innovation. However, monetization of creative endeavours was not the motive. Money and material were not considered the worthiest endeavours.

The heartful leadership, which emphasizes on linking the individuals and societies through a common thread of humanity, helps in understanding that how one relates to the rest of the world for producing greater good. It emphasizes on integration of empathy, morality and spirituality for producing the common-good. In order to transform the education at large, the higher education leaders may find heartfulness focused leadership quite a pragmatic approach. With the Heartful Leadership, our leaders can plan and implement changes in the higher education, which will be based on the optimum integration of modern knowledge creation and dissemination approaches with ethical and moral principles underlying the ancient education system.

Heartful leadership[i], as conceptualized as methodology in context of executive coaching, builds on benefits in terms comprising: Leading with confidence and empathy; inspiring and empowering others; and facing challenges with resilience. Building on the Trait Theory (Barton, 2020; Za Zaccaro et. al. 2004; Zaccaro, 2007) of Leadership, which considers the classical 'Great Man Theory' (Cherry, 2020, Day et. al. 2014; Spector, 2015), a practitioner's perspective[ii] conceptualizes 'heartful leaders' having two necessary traits: first, a cause higher than themselves; and secondly, a commitment to personal sacrifices for the higher cause. This indicates a significant departure from the conventional Western models of leadership emphasizing on need for enhancing corporate performance and thus, establishing leadership beyond the 'manager'. Another similar framework of leader as *Yogi* (Tripathi and Amann, 2017) conceptualizes role of leaders on accomplishing the larger common-good through strong commitment and dedication for higher cause than limiting to the narrower performance focused objectives.

The emergence of modern universities and institutions, which appear to follow more corporatized management structure and philosophy, could be good for enhancing the performance of an academic institution as an organization, but at the same time, presents a contrary approach to the role academic institutions are likely to play for transforming education towards larger goal of sustainability. This is the central idea why we pick the concept of 'heartful leadership' as a model for transforming education and driving sustainability.

Figure 1 presents a conceptual framework of 'heartful leadership' in context of education and sustainability. Based on the conceptual foundations, as explained in the preceding sections, we conceptualize 'heartful leadership' as an approach to lead and transform education towards sustainability. The approach is based on three conceptual foundations:

1. Empathy in education planning and delivery

2. Humanism as a paradigm for driving the leadership vision

3. Leaders as catalyst to create collaborative and participative transformation drive (*Yogis*)

The different scholars, thought leaders, researchers and practitioners have contributed to the book focusing on one or more of the above pillars.

Figure 1: A conceptual framework of Heartful Leadership and Education Linkages

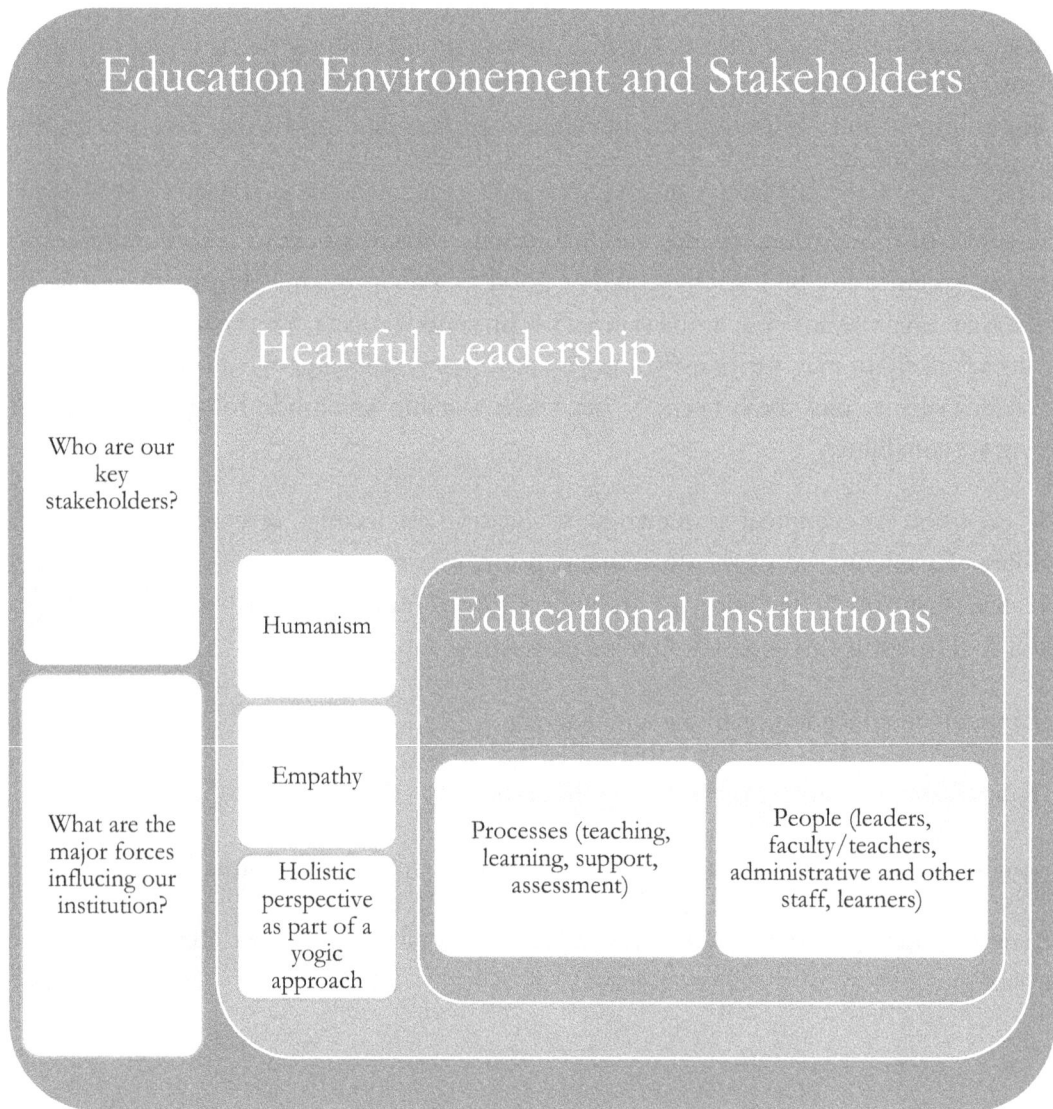

Education Environement and Stakeholders

Heartful Leadership

Who are our key stakeholders?

Humanism

Educational Institutions

Empathy

What are the major forces influcing our institution?

Holistic perspective as part of a yogic approach

Processes (teaching, learning, support, assessment)

People (leaders, faculty/teachers, administrative and other staff, learners)

1.3. Structure of the book

The world is passing through an unprecedented change caused by the global pandemic COVID-19, which has adversely affected the functioning of organizations across sectors and industries. Most of the emerging thoughts, as evident from the thousands of the webinars and opinion articles on the subject, appear to be converging in form of an endorsement on changing role of leadership under the current turbulent environment. To trigger the thought process on the subject, we started with two webinars, first focusing on 'humanism as a driver for responsible healthcare in post COVID-19 situation'[iii] and second on 'heartful leadership for driving desired changes in the education'[iv] to address the emerging challenges. The first webinar highlighted the need for greater 'humanistic orientation' in ensuring the responsible healthcare, which we consider as one of the examples for transforming education. Both the webinars attracted huge participation from different stakeholder groups and accordingly, we decided to develop the concept further by inviting opinions, articles and perspectives from the different stakeholders.

This book captures experience-based propositional knowledge on heartful leadership and its role in transforming education and supporting sustainable development. The contributions in this book mainly address the following issues:

a. What are the conceptual foundations of heartfulness in leadership in the context of educational institutions?

b. What are our experiences as practitioner of heartful leadership in educational institutions?

c. How can heartfulness in leadership be used to transform education at different levels including primary, secondary, vocational and higher education?

d. How can heartfulness in leadership be adopted and aligned in context of higher education institutions (HEIs)?

e. How can heartfulness in leadership become effective when dealing with the required changes in education (pedagogy, mode of delivery, institutional environment, etc.) in post Covid-19 situation?

f. What should be the role of education in fostering humanism and sustainability impact through education, research and training?

g. How can heartful leadership drive education as a catalyst for sustainability?

Wolfgang Amann elaborates heartfulness in leadership with his two chapters early on in this book. First, he reviews in chapter 2 the importance of fostering heartfulness amongst learners. He reasons that this will not be possible without heartfulness leadership among educational leaders who must shape and evolve the most conducive ecosystem for learning. Second, he introduces and discusses in chapter 3 a seven-step model towards the progress. Based on his experience in designing and delivering academic programmes with top rated global business schools, Wolfgang Amann explains why educators must acknowledge and embrace their responsibilities in order to enable the next generation of citizens, leaders, managers and practitioners of all kinds of professions. He stresses why educators, together with learners, must share the duty to design, lead and operate educational institutions that are highly conducive regarding enabling high-impact learning. Building on his scholarly research on learning style versatility, Prof. Amann elaborates how the seven-step model can facilitate learner-centric heartful education management with empathy and humanism as core pillar of the entire process.

Ernst von Kimakowitz links education and heartful leadership to the central theme of 'love and humanism.' In his chapter 4, Dr. Kimakowitz stresses on the five points: first, teaching and learning as two sides of the same coin; second, love for teaching as an essential driver for effective learning in students; third, the reciprocity of teacher learner relationship; fourth, effective learning beyond focus on cognitive capacity; and fifth, appreciation for individuality, dignity and autonomy of each learner. Building on review of literature as well as on his own experiences, Dr. Kimakowitz highlights the uniqueness of the effective teaching-learning through passion and love for the teaching-learning process and thereby, establishing heartful academic leadership.

Dr. Anand Joshi shares in chapter 5 his practitioner focused perspectives on developing heartful leaders in context of education. Drawing insights from Vedic wisdom, Dr. Joshi emphasizes how the transformation process in the education should be aligned to core academic processes of knowledge creation and dissemination. In context of transformative educational leadership, he strongly stresses on combining the spirituality with behavioural intelligence of the leaders for the greater cause of wisdom-focused education.

In chapter 6, Dr. Umesh Mukhi and Mr. Saurabh Saha combines the insights from industry and academia while building an academic entrepreneur perspective on developing heartful leadership. Authors identify a clear gap in understanding and developing 'empathy' in formal leadership development process. Taking the example of executive leadership course, authors agree that the executive education thas the potential to create continuous impact and fill the empathy gap because of the less time span required to apply the concepts. The central idea of this chapter is to outline how empathy can become as essential factor to instill the notion of "Heartful Leadership".

Dr. Deepti Sharma presents in chapter 7 a process-focused model for heartful leadership. The model elaborates the role of care, courage, composure and consciousness as essential driver for heartful leadership, which in turn, enhances the impact through desired quality in teaching-learning. The heartful leadership process is significant for the education, as it also contributes to creativity and innovation and produces the happiness with mental well-being.

Chapter 8 allows Abhilasha Singh to present cornerstones of heartful leadership for the global social good and thereby adopts an action intervention perspective. Based on her experience as an educational leader, she outlines how school such leaders can drive change, improve practices, and create champions in teachers and students alike. She shares how leaders inspire outstanding leadership in others. She links her analysis and recommendations to catalysing sustainable education. Leadership, she argues, is not only about the leaders but the followers and the degree they benefit, grow, and accept their leaders.

Chapter 9 introduces Shalini Chauhan's expertise. Focusing on conveying math skills, this chapter details the crucial role of empathy. It is the prerequisite for gaining credibility and trust. Teachers ought to serve as role models for the next generation and thus perceive their responsibilities not as a job. Empathy can then help understand each learner and adapt the learning journeys. Regularly scheduled moments of truth and monitoring of progress supports teachers in their quest to stay on track. Based on the analysis, the learning environment can benefit from a certain degree of informality as this can foster constructive feedback loops and space for the learners to grow.

Chapter 10 adds the thoughts of Shabnam Siddiqui and Arya Dev to the emerging multifaceted view on heartfulness in educational leadership. The authors and colleagues underline the importane of fighting corruption and increasing transparency. Their moral foundation relies on the United Nations Sustainable Development Goals. The authors argue that during the formative years, learners gain exposure to sustainability issues and hone the skills to manage complexity when building solutions. Building personal resilience is part of this educational journey towards effective citizenship. Finally, chapter 11 presents conclusions – linking the analysis to the two key issues necessitating change in today's education sector. COVID-19 as well as the rise of AI question established solutions so fundamentally, that perpetuating the past will simply not be possible any more.

References

- Barton, E. (2020). Trait leadership theory. https://edbarton.com/topics/leadership/what-is-leadership/trait-leadership-theory/ on 07/24/2020.

- Cherry, K. (2020). The great man theory of leadership. https://www.verywellmind.com/the-great-man-theory-of-leadership-2795311#citation-1

- Day, D., Fleenor, J., & Atwater, L. (2014). Advances in leader and leadership development: A review of 25 years of research and theory. Leadership Quarterly, 25, 63–82.

- Spector, B. (2015). Carlyle, Freud, and the great man theory more fully considered. Leadership, 12(2), 250–260.

- Tripathi, S., & Amann, W. (2017). Corporate Yoga: A primer for sustainable and humanistic leadership. Information Age Publishing.

- Zaccaro, S. J. (2007). Trait-based perspectives of leadership. American Psychologist, 62(1), 6–16.

- Zaccaro, S., Kemp, C., & Bader, P. (2004). Leader traits and attributes. In J. Antonakis, A, Cianciolo, & R. Sternberg (Eds.), The nature of leadership (pp. 134-149). Sage.

Chapter 2: The space for heartfulness in learning taxonomies

Wolfgang Amann

2.1. Introduction to learning to taxonomies

Working in the education sector, be it as a board member of an institution offering all from kindergarten to the International Baccalaureate (IB), serving as executive director or board member at institution at the tertiary education level, I continue to be amazed about the focus on cognitive skills without sufficient emphasis on heartfulness. For example, one of the established models in the learning field is the revised Bloom taxonomy of learning goals or RBT (Anderson et al., 2001). It differentiates six levels of learning and starts with mere remembering in the form of retrieving what is deemed relevant in a field. It continues with understanding in terms of determining what messages stand for. It proceeds to applying in terms of carrying out a task aptly. Next in line is analysing and requires an individual to be able to break down material into various components and detect how there are connected. The model continues with evaluating and foresees judgment and juxtapositions towards checklists and requirements. The model culminates in creating as a task, encouraging an individual to go beyond the known and to form a coherent new solution. The role of heartfulness is limited as the emphasis is on mastering subjects without linking it to purpose.

The Dreyfus learning model (Dreyfus & Dreyfus (1986) does not differ much in this regard. It differentiates five different levels of learning progress. To begin with, a novice at level 1 is required to adhere to rules rather rigidly. This is already a demanding task at this early learning stage. There is no opportunity to apply own discretionary judgement. Subsequently, the advance beginner on level 2 opens up to still rather limited situational perception. Different factors are treated in isolation, often without prioritization. On level 3, the competent learner adopts a more deliberate approach to planning, forms routines, and can sort through various demands and prioritize them. On level 4, the proficient learner is characterized by a more holistic view as he or she recognized more or less importance issues. The learner is able to deviate from the norm with good reasons. Finally, the expert on level 5 goes beyond established rules and, similar to Bloom's model described above, creates newer approaches. Solutions are highly situational. The learner is both visionary and analytical to back up innovations.

A third classic learning model worth mentioning is Kolb's approach to learning via an experiential learning loop (cf. Kolb & Kolb, 2006). Truly skilled teachers or faculty members can start the learning journey at different stages, as long as the loop would eventually be complete. Under normal circumstances, the learning would foresee a concrete experience, ideally a joint one so there is an opportunity for peer learning built in. The teachers or faculty members as learning architects then endeavour to explore these concrete experiences and attached feelings. The learners should then embark on reflective observations. They ought to reflect on what they have worked on, perceived, and gained from it. The learning cycle moves on to a more abstract conceptualization of the learnings. The learner should distil principles and hands-on insights from the practical efforts. Eventually, the learner should then receive the opportunity to actively experiment with these new insights. They should act on them, apply, experiment, and practice.

Once more, however, learning seems to be too value-free or value-neutral. This chapter, in turn, argues for a more elaborate integration of value and in particular heartfulness into learning taxonomies. The analysis continues by zooming in on one contemporary learning taxonomy to elaborate on this train of thought. The chapter then continues on resulting leadership development needs to take heartfulness forward in educational institutions.

2.2. Integrating heartfulness in learning taxonomies

As outlined in the following table, there is a variety of approaches to learning taxonomies. They include earlier approaches as Bloom's (1956) model as well as more recent ones as suggested, for example, by Viji and Benedict (2017). These authors emphasize latest technologies realities, which allow learners to be online continuously. As they are able to be online and could look up mere facts or figures, studying them by heart becomes less critical when compared with higher order cognitive accomplishments, such as ingenuity.

Table 1: Timeline of selected educational taxonomies

Year	Title	Features
1956	Bloom's taxonomy	Cognitive, affective and psychomotor
1979	Experiential taxonomy	Exposure, participation, identification, internalisation, dissemination
1982	SOLO (Structure of Observed Learning Outcomes) taxonomy	Pre-structural, uni-structural, multi-structural, relational, extended abstract
1989	Mc Cormack and Yager's taxonomy	Knowledge, process, creativity, application, attitude

1990	Revised Bloom's taxonomy	Remembering, understanding, applying, analysing, evaluating, creating
2000	Marzano's new taxonomy	Knowledge, cognitive system, metacognitive system, self-system
2001	Anderson et al.'s taxonomy	Factual, conceptual, procedural, and metacognitive knowledge
2003	Fink's taxonomy	Foundational knowledge, application, integration, human dimension, caring, learning how to learn
2007	Bloom's digital taxonomy	Remembering, understanding, applying, analysing, evaluating, creating
2017	Viji and Benedict's taxonomy	Emphasizing 21st century learning skills, ingenuity, connectedness and a local context

Source: Extending Viji and Benedict (2017, p. 193)

One particular well established model has been put forward by Marzano (2000). He moves beyond traditional learning taxonomies to distinguishes three systems put into a clear hierarchy:

- Most importantly, the self-system addresses the beliefs about how crucial a particular field and learning about it is. It equally clarifies the beliefs about one's efficacy and sheds light on knowledge-related affections.

- Subsequently, the taxonomy explores the metacognition system on the level below, which also can be referred to as "mission control". It tackles preferred learning goals.

- The third cognitive system deals with the retrieval of once learnt knowledge, different degrees of comprehension, profound analysis, and knowledge utilisation.

Heartfulness is not as explicitly integrated into this taxonomy as it could and should be. This taxonomy, however, is particularly holistic as it adds these three systems on top of regular knowledge domain. Heartfulness can be integrated into the most important self-system. If the why is clear, the how is easy. If the learner understands and agrees with the purpose of a subject and learning more about it, he or she will embrace it even more, deem investments in ongoing learning more rewarding than this would otherwise be the case and as a consequence, motivation to continue learning will remain at higher level for a more extended period of time. The analysis can be taken further. If we cultivate more warm-hearted learners, hitherto impossible quantities and qualities of learning motivations can be reached. Individuals caring, for example, about sustainability would not shy away from its otherwise easily overwhelming complexity.

This purpose-orientation cascades down to the second system of metacognition which deals with learning strategies. Those with an intrinsic motivation to learn about a topic would apply more diligence and sophisticated learning strategies to learn how to master a subject.

On the cognitive system below can be split into four parts – retrieval, comprehension, analysis, and knowledge utilization. To name but one example, knowledge utilization includes own investigations into a subject. This is where an individual could search for additional insights beyond what is offered in the classroom – an invaluable step towards more independence and mastery. Yet, this step requires more than just mindfulness of what might matter in a field. It necessitates a strong sense of caring about stakeholders and higher degrees of heartfulness.

2.3. Resulting development needs for institutional leaders

Working with the Marzano (2000) learning taxonomy, an ideal type of learner emerges. He or she self-orients, self-motivates, self-trains, and self-develops when it comes to learning activities and links gains in learning efficiency and effectiveness to values. Heartfulness prescribes a strong sense of responsibility and commitment towards stakeholder, not isolated ego-centric greed to name but one example.

Such ideal learners would not become possible without a conducive learning environment, which in turn is the full responsibility of institutional leaders. In my research, national and organizational culture matters as much as the individual quality of institutional leaders and instructors. National culture could foresee a variety seniority-oriented, hierarchical setting, which could cause learners to restrict themselves to passive roles. Organizational culture can shape realities as well. Private organizations can lead to an exaggerated profit orientation and poor learning experiences as funds are taken out of the system instead of invested into learning. A private set-up could also see leaders creating differentiated services and thus the exact opposite reality. Eventually, it all boils down to the right type of leader. Is someone able to balance multiple demands? Is an individual in the education sector to help form winners and well-trained graduates with promising profiles? This requires heartfulness on the side of institutional leaders. They should build on their intrinsic motivation to serve, to educate, to enable, to empower, to enrich and to continuously learn how to do so better. Inevitably, educational leaders are learners. As their environment changes and as demands evolve, they ought to never rest on their laurels and learn how to better their services and impact. They should thus be able to design, direct, and implement sound organizational change projects accordingly.

They should keep abreast of latest developments in the field of learning, not necessarily jumping blindly on any fad but modernize proactively. One of the emerging insights in the education sector is that mere knowledge would clearly not suffice any longer. Millo and Schinckus (2016) proposed a helpful set of semantics relying on ancient Greek thinking. As the following figure illustrates, they differentiate between five main learning fields. Episteme is more theoretical knowledge while sophia emphasizes the theoretical ways on how to gain more of it from a wisdom perspective. The education sector often deals with preparing the future generation of practitioners, which is depicted in the bottom half of the following visualization. Here, techne refers to all technical knowledge – the numbers, facts and figures in a field as well as the core skills to build solutions.

Figure 2: Overview of learning fields

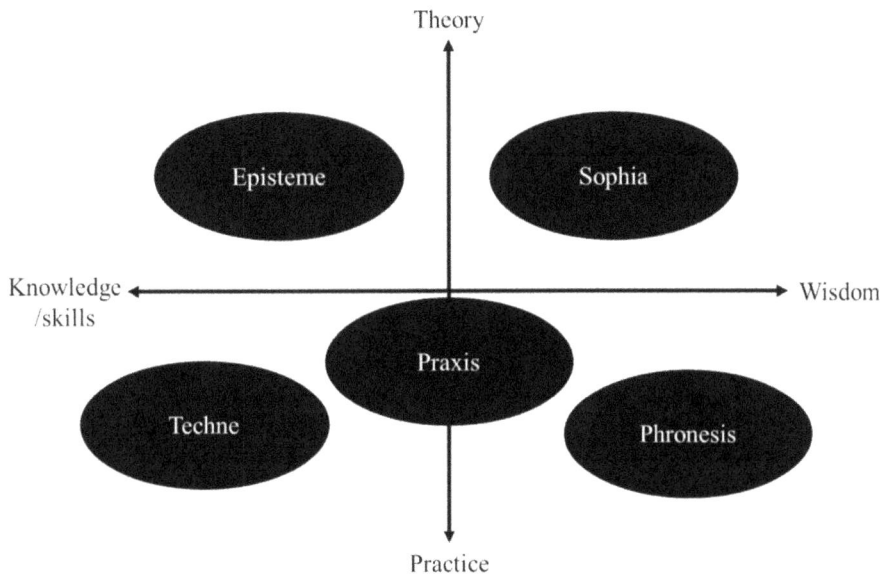

Source: Based on Millo and Schinckus (2016)

Praxis, in turn, is a at a different level. It relates more to overarching principles without getting too detailed on either the technical knowledge or skills. These principles help in cases of ambiguity. Recently, phronesis as practical wisdom gained more importance. What should math be good for? Why still study Latin? Why pursue general education tracks? Practical wisdom is situational, value-oriented, and aiming at temporary solutions only as environments continue to change. This is the big difference when compared to Aristotle's concept of phronesis 1.0. In his dated view, practical wisdom can be built over decades, would always allow one to know precisely what to do in a given case based on rational choice and all individuals should pursue such an accumulation of experience as the foundation of wisdom. As a consequence, the phronimons, i.e. the practically wise person, can then cope with any presented situation.

A more modern concept of phronesis 2.0, however, breaks with the assumption that it takes decades to build practical wisdom. Today's graduate and will not have the that much time! Today's VUCA world can also not be analysed as easily. Complex situation resits a logic analysis. Today, the phronimos needs to embrace issues with a beginner's mind mentality instead of decades old and thus dated experiences.

The following figure sheds light on the process. In my research on building practical wisdom, six Cs emerge as crucial. Like in a duolog set-up in a theatre two actors play crucial parts. The instructor can contribute three distinct activities to foster a highly conducive learning environment. Calibrating requires the instructor, be it teacher or faculty member, to tailor the course and the learning experience to the target group. It should matter who sits in in the physical or virtual room. The instructor must serve multiple learning styles and as there is ambiguity about preferences and actual abilities to learn in a certain way, the instructor cannonades. Multiple and divergent learning methods find their application to increase the likelihood of one hitting a specific target. The learning process continues with a distinct effort to really impact the learner significantly as part of a truly transformational learning experience. Learning should be over when this impact is done, not when the time of a class session is up.

Figure 3: The 6C–duolog theory on building practical wisdom

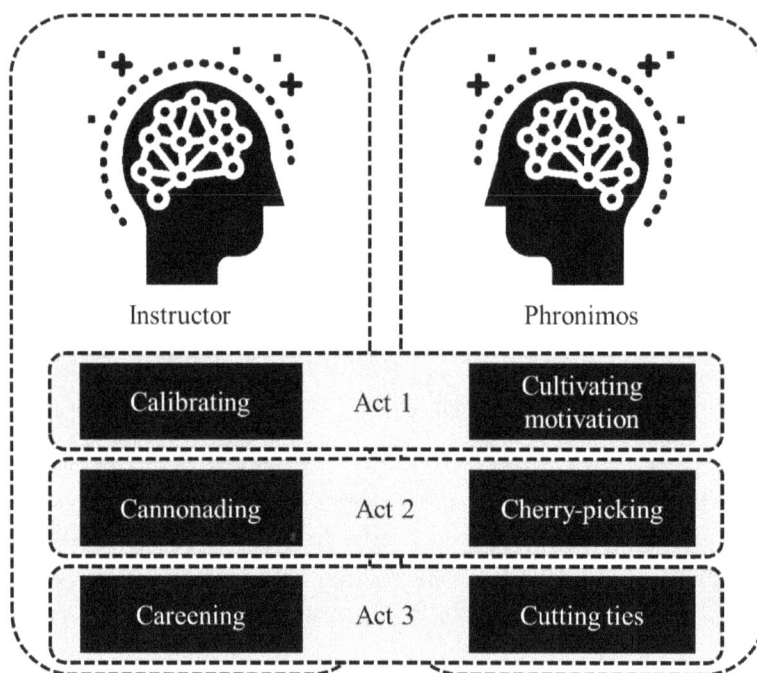

Instructor		Phronimos
Calibrating	Act 1	Cultivating motivation
Cannonading	Act 2	Cherry-picking
Careening	Act 3	Cutting ties

But not all responsibility is on the instructor. The aspiring phronimos, i.e., the learner, must work and evolve the motivation to learn. Too frequently, there is a mentality of pursuing degrees or learning for the exams only. They can discover and amplify their intrinsic motivation, especially when they realize their purpose and the purpose of learning. As the instructor stimulates them with many and different means, they in turn must cherry-pick what would work best for them. Some benefit from a great lecture. Others would deem a simulation or lively case discussion more useful. Finally, the learner will also realize that learning will ultimately be only their responsibility. They cannot forever depend on the instructor to tell them what to do, what to learn and how to do so. They must become independent and drive their own learning.

Needless to say, focusing on practical wisdom represents substantially higher value. It also is not a value-free learning journey as value judgments are an integral part of the resulting practical wisdom. Building such an eco-system requires heartfulness amongst institutional leaders. It is not primarily a question of working at a resource-rich institution. The salaries for the instructors and institutional leaders are paid for already. Few additional investments, if any, are needed for the willing institutional leader to constantly evolve their learning institution. Truly heartful educational leaders would also not compromise these unique learning experiences. They would evolve once found solution over time based on gathered feedback. They would spot and develop faculty talent. They would share best practices. Their organizations would be role models, which for the case of business schools is prescribed by the addendum principle of the Principles of Responsible Management Education as part of the United Nations Global Compact initiative. Educational leaders should not shy away from the complexity and the efforts needed. Heartfulness would fuel their constant and never-ending improvements.

2.4. Conclusions

This chapter presents the reader with a moment of reflection. Do we know sufficiently about the learning models? Are we aware of the ways we can enrich them with values? How to ensure we not only form graduate that are efficient and effective but link their knowledge and skills to the right purpose? An argument is made in this chapter that heartfulness amongst learners is the consequence of heartfulness amongst educational leaders. Their organizations are a shadow of themselves. They imprint their organizations with their own values. They set the right examples and priorities.

References

- Anderson, L., Krathwohl, D., Airasian, P., Cruikshank, K., Mayer, R., Pintrich, P., Raths, J., & Wittrock, M. (Eds.). (2001). A taxonomy for learning, teaching, and assessing: A revision of Bloom's taxonomy of educational objectives. Allyn & Bacon.

- Bloom, B. (1956). Taxonomy of educational objectives: the classification of educational goals. Longmans.

- Dreyfus, H., & Dreyfus, S. (1986). Mind over Machine: The Power of Human Intuition and Expertise in the Era of the Computer. Oxford, Basil Blackwell.

- Kolb, A., & Kolb, D. (2006) Learning styles and learning spaces: A review of the multidisciplinary application of experiential learning theory in higher education. In R. R. Sims & S. J. Sims (Eds.), Learning styles and learning: A key to meeting the accountability demands in education (pp. 45–91). Nova Science.

- Marzano, R. (2000). Designing a new taxonomy of educational objectives. Corwin Press.

- Millo, Y., & Schinckus, C. (2016). A nuanced perspective on episteme and techne in finance. International Review of Financial Analysis, 46, 124–130.

- Viji, V., & Benedict, K. (2017). Conceptualization of an Innovative Educational Taxonomy for the 21st Century Learners. https://files.eric.ed.gov/fulltext/ED578106.pdf.

Chapter 3: Heartfulness – seven steps towards progress

Wolfgang Amann

3.1. Introduction

Before starting my work in higher education, I studied in Switzerland where, 200 years ago, Johann Heinrich Pestalozzi was already having a huge impact on education across Europe. A Swiss social reformer and educator, he became known as the father of modern education. Some scholars argue that it was Pestalozzi who established education as a separate field of knowledge besides, for example, politics. He cared greatly for the underprivileged and poor, worrying about just how useful or useless their education had been. He strongly advocated growth opportunities along the three dimensions of head, heart and hands. In short, education should provide them with a cool head, warm heart and working hands.

The natural, yet holistic, outcome of his educational philosophy, which embraced the interest and needs of children, not their teachers, was of primary importance. This honest, authentic learner-centeredness penetrates the entire learning experience that he advocated. It fosters learners' freedom to self-actualise, experience more directly and to provide a holistic education, which might well involve more coordinated efforts with other stakeholders - during his time, the parents.

While I was the academic director of programs at one of the best business schools in the world, Pestalozzi's guidance on education remained as inspiring and relevant as ever, and, even better, complied with the KISS approach for strategic success – Keep It Simple, Stupid. The U.S. navy originally coined the term in 1960 as a design principle and recurs also more diplomatically as: keep it simple, not simplistic. Those who help form graduates and undertake the research that helps them do this should aspire to have a cool head, warm heart, and working hands.

The cool head refers to proper thinking techniques and a critical degree of emotional intelligence that one needs to acquire and hone during one's formative years. Graduates ought to become more aware of their emotions and those of others. They ought to learn how to manage, not manipulate, these emotions more effectively and not ignore them. In our time when artificial intelligence and digitalisation are taking over many data analyses and processing tasks, emotional intelligence and the ability to practice sound judgement with a cool head - no matter the crisis or the problems' degree of wickedness - become key.

The warm heart aspect refers to heartfulness, which should grow in parallel. Globally and locally, signs of unsustainability are increasing. For example, the Covid-19 crisis, which started haunting the world in early 2020, made the rich richer and decreased equality and equity. The educational and career opportunities of many students received a knock with schools closing temporarily or they had to struggle with online delivery modes. It takes heartful individuals to first return to the previous levels of sustainability before aspiring to go beyond these.

Working hands points to the practical relevance of education, which Pestalozzi already criticised in the educational systems he encountered some 200 years ago. Societal and workplace change's speed and scope currently add to the topic's complexity. To illustrate this point, the World Economy Forum[v] predicts that more than 20% of jobs currently in place globally will be redundant by 2022, that at this time, 27% of the jobs will be a new type and that only a minority of jobs will be stable. The World Economic Forum also predicts that only a minority of roles would not require the people filling them to be reskilled. 30% of jobs would need multi-month reskilling initiatives, nor merely a few days or weeks of training. These challenges impose increasing burdens on the educational sector. The China-based billionaire and founder of Alibaba, Jack Ma, calls for the educational sector to be revolutionised, because traditional graduates simply won't be able to compete effectively with AI.

At the start of my current courses, I give students a brief exercise: I show them a slide with 1500 penguins drawn in icon style. All of them are identical, with the exception of one, whose nose is not top down, but bottom up. I ask them to identify the anomaly. This usually takes a moment. Only a few students, perhaps 5% of a class of 30-year-old students eventually find this penguin within three minutes. Most can't and give up. They experience an aha-moment when I tell them that an AI application can identify this anomaly within a second – even without knowing what the anomaly is. An AI application learns patterns and spots the case that violates its self-learned design principles. This leads the students to acknowledge that they must have different skills, that these have to add unique value and that they need to exhibit more than basic information absorption and processing skills. They have to learn that they need a cool head to cut through complexity, need to have a warm heart to design and implement more sustainable, humanistic solutions, and need to achieve results effectively.

Educators must acknowledge and embrace their responsibilities in order to enable the next generation of citizens, leaders, managers and practitioners of all kinds of professions. Together with the learner, educators share the duty to design, lead and operate educational institutions that are highly conducive regarding enabling high-impact learning. The United Nations' Global Compact initiative's Principles of Responsible Management Education (PRME) phrases this role very elegantly in its addendum principle: Institutions have to be role models of what they want others to accomplish. They have to walk the talk. The business education sector or 'industry' needed this extra guidance when faced with their alumni's many scandals and because they acknowledged that businesses are a major transmission belt for more sustainable, humanistic societies. The insight that institutions ought to be role models and walk the talk is currently universally valid. Mahatma Gandhi phrased this aptly when stating: Be the change you want to see in the world. This chapter illustrates how educational institutions can live up to the standards they (should) set for their learners by outlining how they can approach heartfulness in their setting and bring it to life.

The following sections introduce various steps towards this goal. They are an eclectic set of priorities based on my experience of leading initiatives in the educational sector, of learning from top schools, from various teacher programs that I attended and later designed, directed and taught. These steps should be understood as a source of inspiration and encouragement to critically reflect on one's situation and solutions. They need to be adapted to local settings and needs, forming part of a local, holistic learning experience rather than representing standardised, abstract ideas.

At the same time, they form part of a logical sequence of questions for practitioners: Where to start, how to proceed and how to progress towards measuring success. Initial thoughts on embracing a learner's individuality help us start the analysis. However, before commencing with the proposed steps towards more heartfulness, I briefly explain the understanding underlying the concept.

3.2. Mindfulness versus heartfulness

Mindfulness has become a rather hip concept, and in line with Pestalozzi's quest to utilise the mind more aptly. Originally based on insights he gained in India, it was Jon Kabit-Zinn who popularised the concept in the West. He adapted the concept in 1979 when designing his Mindful-Based Stress Reduction Programme to make it more marketable in the West. He originally targeted individuals who failed to respond well to medication. Mindfulness helped a patient on the path towards emotional intelligence. It also increases awareness of one's attention, actual purpose, balance issues and potential judgment biases. It fosters understanding and, more than before, truly understanding what is on one's mind.

Conversely, heartfulness is not primarily about what is on one's mind, but what is on one's heart. The concepts overlap with regard to the attention they pay to what constitutes a better focus. Mindfulness encourages worrying less about the past or the future. More mindfulness can help reduce stress or the waste of energy when lost thinking about worse case scenarios in endless loops of worrying. It can improve memory, balance, health and relationships. Mindfulness requires shifting attention, practice and learning, therefore requiring time and commitment. It is not something that can be ordered from a menu at a restaurant and received passively some 15 minutes later. Heartfulness shares many of these features and the overall need for patience.

Beyond this congruence with heartfulness in this regard, complementing what is on the mind with what is on the heart can lead to more holistic growth. It necessitates revisiting the rational, brain-heavy thinking within learning but also in organisational development, which the anti-humanistic scientific management movement and Taylorism fostered strongly for more than 100 years. This chapter is about encouraging rethinking of how to lead and organise in the educational sector. It redirects attention and energy to the core motives and ends with forming the next generation of citizens and graduates. The chapter helps reorient the compass of institutional leaders and of those who orchestrate learning journeys in classrooms more directly.

3.3. Key steps in advancing heartfulness in education

When it comes to linking leadership, organisational development and learning with rediscovered heartfulness, the field might well need more innovation, frameworks, best and worse practice cases and peer exchanges to learn from and advance. This chapter builds on decades-long experience in the field but remains at the propositional knowledge level. The following steps might need adaptation to specific situations and represent an invitation to fellow educators and institutional leaders to create their own answers to how to best embrace and bring heartfulness to life before they evolve the concept and their solutions further over time.

Step 1: Establish and protect the right values within the organisational culture

From research on strategically directing and developing organisations[vi], we learn that:

- There is often no consistent way of describing strategy

- Departments are misaligned in more than 75% of cases

- There is frequently no link between strategy and budgets

- Incentives are mostly not linked to strategy

- Strategy often lacks understanding – it is not uncommon for 95% of staff members not to know what their institution or organisation's strategy is

- Strategy is insufficiently communicated, because about 85% of organisational leaders spend less than one hour per month discussing and explaining their overall direction.

Each organisation is, of course, unique, might have very effective leaders in place or lack them. Each educational institution has its idiosyncrasies. Nevertheless, the statistics above warns of potential pitfalls. Very senior leaders might well be perfectly acquainted with the organisational direction, because their big picture perspective, involvement in setting the direction, access to better information and responsibilities in the institutional hierarchy ensure they have more opportunities to gain clarity. This does not apply to mid-level or lower-level staff members. These employees have a different focus and, as we have observed, need frequent communication about the organisational direction.

This is by no means an inevitable situation. There are many communication and communication reinforcement tools, and means with which to clarify the organisational purpose, direction and values, ranging from image brochures, website texts, town hall meetings and posters on hallway walls. Repetition and alignment ensure that the core messages and values are not only received, but also effectively brought to life. The programme brochures should repeat the educational goals and values on their first page, such as heartfulness. Programme directors ought to reinforce the right values throughout their meetings and over years. When making decisions, leaders, such as programme directors or section heads, should prepare for and justify their decisions by repeatedly referring to the pursued values.

The right values also need to be established and implemented appropriately. In this context, we usually distinguish between three types of values. Firstly, there are those that should never be compromised. Violating them must have strong disciplinary or other social repercussions to set standards and align future behaviours. In this book, we argue in favour of warm-heartedness or heartfulness as a value - perhaps even a core value – that should never be compromised. The number of core values needs to be small. If an organisation has a whole list of core values, it might as well have none. Many core values merely confuse people. Secondly, deviations from other values need to be explained and cannot occur without a strong reason. Suspension can, as an exception, make sense and be tolerated as long as it can be sufficiently justified. Thirdly, there are various nice-to-have values that could be applied if conditions permit. Allowing students and staff more leeway to observe them can act as a bottom-up innovation catalyst and foster positive organisational energies. Put more colloquially, these values can make the organisation more fun, since not everything is perfectly regulated from the top down in a highly rigid bureaucracy.

Step 2: Acknowledging individualism via learning styles and learning style versatility

Nicely formatted value posters on hallway walls and similar materials could never sufficiently foster heartfulness in educational institutions. In practice, these institutions risk a knowing-doing gap, with the organisational leaders and staff members knowing the ideal values, but not linking them to action. Consequently, it is very important to design concrete steps to actually implement heartfulness. Acknowledging the individuality of each and every learner is one of the first ways to embrace heartfulness. All learners are unique, have their own individual strength profiles and learning needs, and often have very personal agendas.

When designing and running schools, academies, colleagues, universities, executive education boutiques or vocational training institutions, organisational leaders and teachers might be easily overwhelmed by having to comply with a variety of demands, such as fulfilling regulations, observing budgets, delivering the curriculum, managing emergencies and crises as well as their own lives, which includes managing their personal growth, careers, leisure time interests, health, relationships as well as their family and societal responsibilities.

The following figure illustrates that, in more modern approaches to educational philosophies, learners receive a more pronounced freedom to think critically and to be themselves. While perennialism views the teacher as the source of wisdom and the learner as mere passive recipients, education can also unfold differently. Essentialism, for example, links education to the level beyond the single teacher and clarifies education's role in society. Education can reproduce the social strata and culture. However, today's fast-paced technological change, globalisation influences and the rise of individualism, to name but a few trends, question the rather rigidity-enhancing essentialist approach to education.

In turn, progressivism acknowledges that learning is on the rise, although not in terms of eternal truths, but focused on dilemmas in order to hone critical thinking and problem-solving skills. Forcing learners to study topics by heart is simply insufficient. From a Reconstructionist view of education, societies are expected and even encouraged to change over time. Today's sustainability changes and changing job profiles require a more fundamental and revolutionary approach to education. Learning should be more situational, tailored and relative to what is needed in each case. In should no longer be about the teacher's or faculty member's communication needs. Knowledge is clearly no longer absolute.

Figure 4: Students' and faculty members' divergent educational philosophies identified in this study

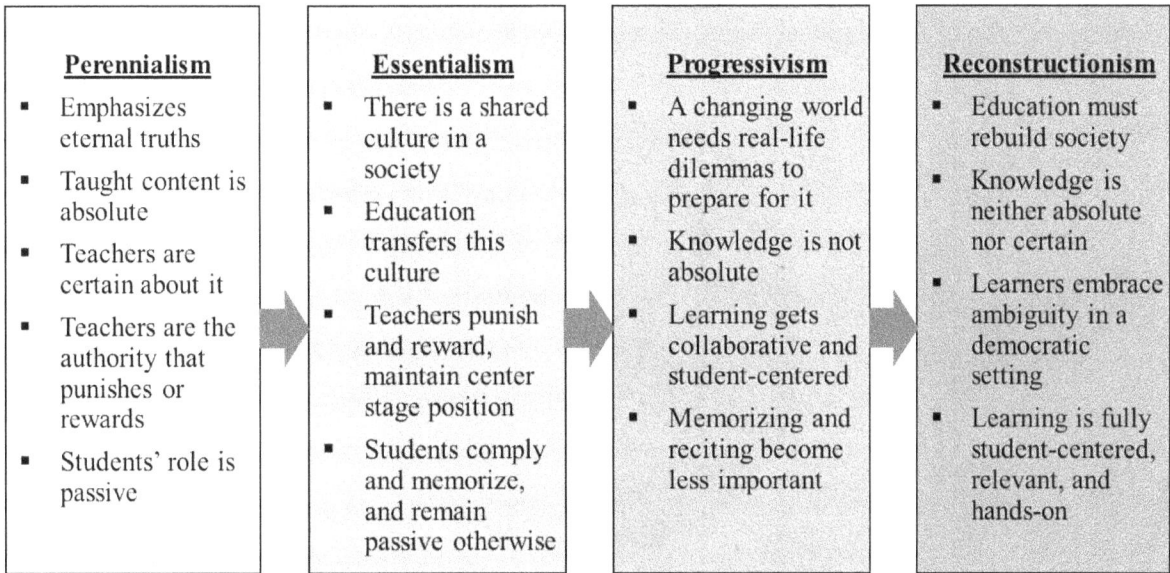

Perennialism	**Essentialism**	**Progressivism**	**Reconstructionism**
• Emphasizes eternal truths • Taught content is absolute • Teachers are certain about it • Teachers are the authority that punishes or rewards • Students' role is passive	• There is a shared culture in a society • Education transfers this culture • Teachers punish and reward, maintain center stage position • Students comply and memorize, and remain passive otherwise	• A changing world needs real-life dilemmas to prepare for it • Knowledge is not absolute • Learning gets collaborative and student-centered • Memorizing and reciting become less important	• Education must rebuild society • Knowledge is neither absolute nor certain • Learners embrace ambiguity in a democratic setting • Learning is fully student-centered, relevant, and hands-on

Source: Based on Bolat and Bas (2018)

This is where the actual acknowledgment of a learner's individuality enters the fray. This acknowledgment can be conceptualised and operationalised practically with the help of learning style measurements. This approach truly puts learning and the learner first. It clarifies that the learning process comprises – in one of the many possible views – an information perception part and an information processing part. In terms of the perceived information phase, a learner might have a preference for a rather abstract way of perceiving information or, alternatively, an inclination towards a rather concrete perception. With regard to information processing, an individual might make more progress if there is an element that encourages active experimentation or, conversely, more reflection.

Consequently, and as shown in the following, several types of dominant learning styles emerge. The following figure illustrates these styles along the perception and processing phases' two dimensions. Each class is likely to show a distinct distribution of styles.

Figure 5: Sample distribution of learners across dominant learning styles

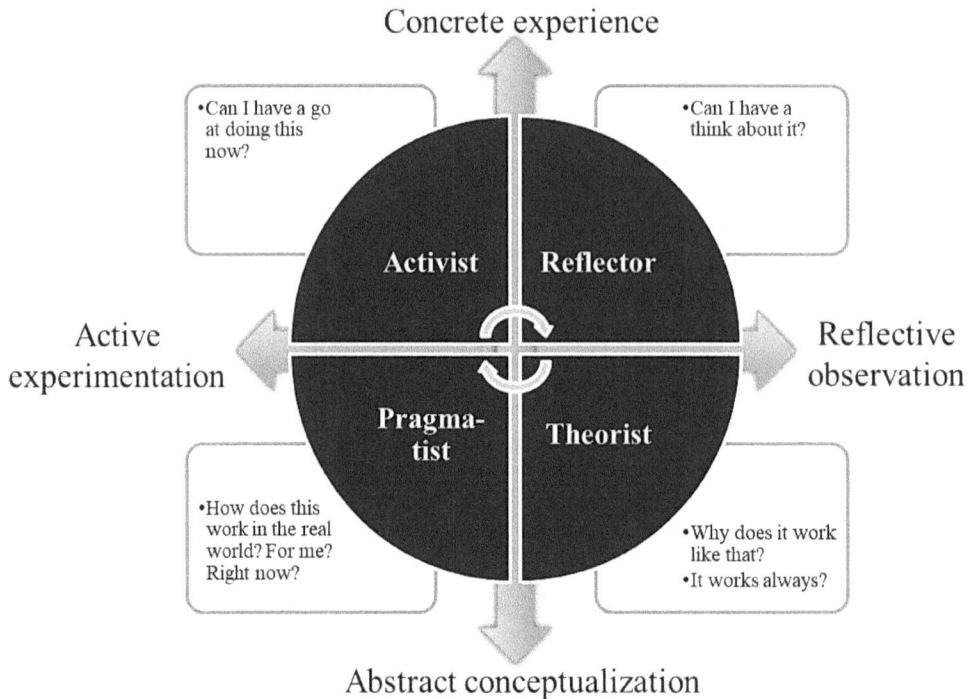

As shown in the figure above, the learning style questionnaire (LSQ) outlined by Duff and Duffy (2002) identifies four main types of learners. The activist prefers to gain experiences, the reflector learns through observation and reflection, the theorist relies on frameworks, concepts, facts and figures while, last but not least, the pragmatist learns by simplifying and reducing learning to the absolute essentials – the few points that need to be retained or to be done better or differently.

According to the meshing hypothesis, learning is optimised when a course's delivery style corresponds to a learner's preferences and strengths. If students are challenges to learn in modes they are not used to or comfortable with, this by no means equals total learning failure, since learning can still occur.

However, the learning style field has for a long time ignored any versatility orientation. This versatility is not only about making the class participants and teachers more aware of their learning style preferences or about consciously complying with or temporarily ignoring styles in order to access new learning stimuli. The field is progressing towards prioritising learning style versatility beyond learning styles. As outlined in the following figure, learner profiles differ, and they can exhibit a preference for a lower or a higher degree of learning style versatility. Scores gathered in learning style surveys include raw scores, relative scores to larger peer groups and an individual assessment of learning preferences as either very low, low, moderate, strong or very strong.

Learner A has only one learning style preference and strength. He or she is an activist who learns less effectively in a typical lecture-based class with a one-way communication from the teacher to him or her. The learner is more likely to struggle, learn less and to find the teacher or class boring and ineffective. Dissatisfied students are three times likelier to complain and not be good school ambassadors than a happy learner.

Learner B is strong in reflection and pragmatism. He or she learns best if there is space to think, either in a more or less guided way. Yet, merely pushing a lot of content and keeping him or her overly busy miss the point of learning. He or she needs reduced pragmatic advice on what to focus – not extensive preludes, many readings, slides and exercises.

Learner C might well count as a very positive case. He or she learns naturally in different modes. Research carried out at HEC Paris provided quantitative evidence that greater learning style versatility leads to better classroom performance, learning and actual grades. Learner C learns well via reflection, theories, and concepts as well as through practical advice. He or she does not need much practice or experimenting to understand and function more effectively in future.

The absolute core question is therefore: which learning style versatility profile would enable a learner to best cope with a variety of learning challenges across different subjects, such as math, history, geography, etc., or to later cope with tertiary education's diverse courses? Similarly, which learning style versatility would better allow the learner to cope with a job and with life when careers and changing job profiles require learning, unlearning, and relearning? The answer is rather straightforward: more versatile learners should adapt more easily and learn more effectively from a variety of learning opportunities. As outlined in the introduction, the World Economic Forum maintains that, within the next few years, the majority of jobs will demand reskilling, while others will disappear, or might not yet be invented.

Heartfulness in education requires attention to the differences in learning styles and learning style versatility, because these differences and versatility respect human dignity, a learner's individuality and prepares learners better for an ever-changing life and job market. How learning style versatility could actually be honed depends greatly on the educational philosophy, the talent and ambitions available in an educational institution and on its supporting resources. However, all of the former start with outlining the avenues to start with and to prioritise. Within heartfulness, an orientation towards learning style individuality and versatility is a crucial first step. This orientation adds substantially greater value to not only convey hard skills in math, accounting or engineering, but to also enable individuals to learn how to learn and become more versatile.

Figure 6: Sample learner profiles with varying degrees of learning style versatility

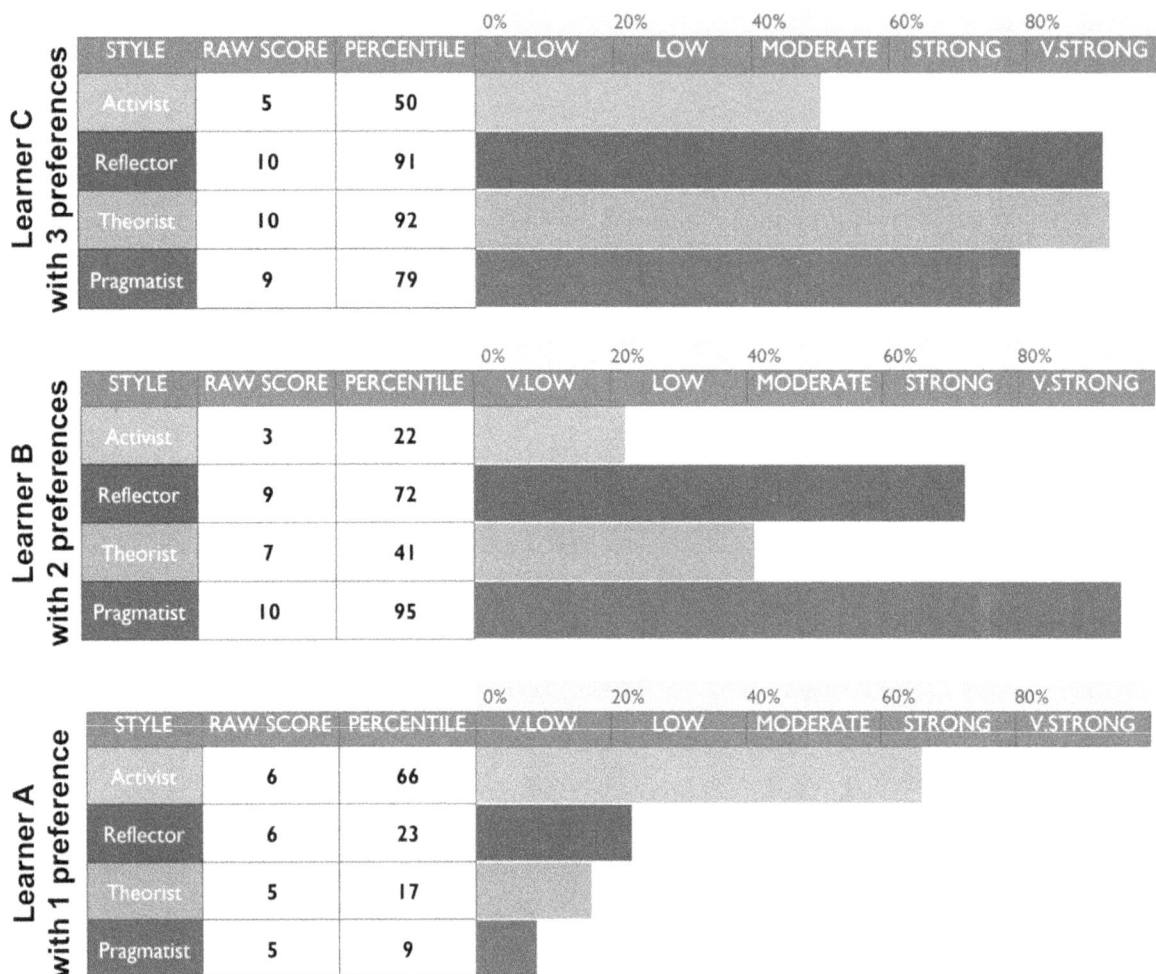

Learner C with 3 preferences

STYLE	RAW SCORE	PERCENTILE
Activist	5	50
Reflector	10	91
Theorist	10	92
Pragmatist	9	79

Learner B with 2 preferences

STYLE	RAW SCORE	PERCENTILE
Activist	3	22
Reflector	9	72
Theorist	7	41
Pragmatist	10	95

Learner A with 1 preference

STYLE	RAW SCORE	PERCENTILE
Activist	6	66
Reflector	6	23
Theorist	5	17
Pragmatist	5	9

A word of caution is required to put this section in context. I mention learning style versatility, which is currently one of the major learning innovations. Marzano and Kendall (2007), for example, view learning as a process that first engages the self-system. This is where learners decide whether to embrace a task or not, where the level of engagement and commitment emerge. Honing learners' learning style versatility can catapult actual learning to unprecedented heights, because the more versatile learners should find it easier – either consciously or more latently – to tackle a new field, trigger sufficient activation to get started and to perpetuate their momentum and motivation to continue their learning process. Even the more recent learning taxonomies, such those by Marzano and Kendall (2007) do not cover learning style versatility explicitly, although they do shift the attention to this self-system before the learning goals and strategies follow on the metacognition level. Even below the metacognition system and level, a learner would deal with the actual knowledge- and skill-related competencies that are formed as part of the cognitive system. Teachers and faculty members are encouraged to acknowledge the individuality of each learner as part of their journey towards more heartfulness. However, these actors are likewise asked to continue updating their understanding of how the field of learning is evolving. There is a likelihood of new concepts, which could advance learning and progress towards heartfulness, continuing to emerge.

Step 3: Adding more value by covering all learning levels

The last section already started triggering more debate on the adding of value. This train of thought is based on two foundations. One is that during the Covid-19 crisis, a number of institutions' costs regarding technological adaptations, training and re-organising increased, while fees, tuition, funding and donation opportunities were limited. The second foundation is based on Datar et al.'s (2010) argument that the field of learning's advances and leverages actually point to frequent shortcomings. Their reasoning regarding business education can be generalised beyond the tertiary level of education and the field of business. These colleagues acknowledge that learning should be multi-levelled, but frequently isn't. However, if it were to be multi-levelled, its balance and emphasis might well be inadequate.

As visualised in the following figure, learning often starts with and is most easily accomplished at the 'knowing' level, comprising the core facts and figures, tangible insights, concepts and frameworks. This knowledge level is easily captured in slides, articles, textbooks, fact sheets, YouTube videos and other online resources. However, the knowledge level is highly insufficient if conveyed without the other levels.

Figure 7: Rendering learning holistic

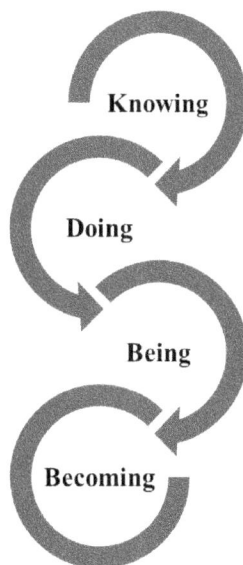

Source: Based on Datar et al. (2010)

The doing level addresses the actual skills required to apply the learnt lessons correctly on the knowledge level in order to solve problems. The skills required to apply lesson learnt soundly ought to be honed differently. They not only have to be linked to the knowledge level, but also to the relevant application possibilities in the real world in order to add value. Learning will always be more effective if not only gained for a potential future use, but also for concrete purposes that are obvious to both the teacher and learner.

The being level appears next in this learning levels framework. Merely teaching about a field and tools or learning how to apply a toolkit are again insufficient. Learning needs to include progress regarding the insight into what kind of citizen and professional in the job market students aspire to be. Is it sufficient to merely reproduce society and dominant cultural elements or should one aspire to be more transformational and transcendental? Does an individual believe that he or she is insignificant in the larger scheme of things and that happiness can be found through detachment or through a belief in the afterlife, or what kind of architect, accountant, soldier, politician or teacher does this individual want to be? What kind of values does this person harbour and what kind of impact does he or she want to make? Such critical reflections at the right level are an essential part of education.

Finally, the level of reflection is key as part of a learning journey. Are leaders born or made? What does social mobility and career advancements require over time? What learning, unlearning and relearning will be required over a lifetime? Educational institutions might well have their limitations when it comes to subject matter strengths. They must pay attention to human growth over time – not necessarily provide predefined answers, but should allow the individual reflection, inspiration and critical thinking required for students to make their own choices. Covering these four levels is essential and forms part of value created in a more heartful approach to education.

Step 4: Measuring success holistically and transparently

How often and how holistically do we actually measure learning? Are the grade averages sufficient? Are our minds to peace if a particular class or school does reasonably well in cross-institutional tests or should our aspirations be higher? When pursuing more ambitious optimised learning goals, it is essential to know where to start and to measure our progress. Phillips (2003) extended previously suggested ways to evaluate learning, which included satisfaction surveys, learning progress and knowledge transfer tests, actual behavioural change, and learning's non-financial impact on employers, with his view on a return on education. Private organisations are, after all, increasing in the education field, which is often also interpreted as an 'industry'.

In this chapter, a crucial addition is required. We call for much more transformational and unique learning experiences, particularly in the heartfulness dimension, which not only affects learners' minds, but also their hearts. Based on deep caring about learners, tailored transformational experiences ought to be designed, directed, implemented and measured quantitatively to map their progress. The latter should obviously keep the learners' age and level in each setting into account.

The following, for example, describes how a class of business students at the graduate level actually learned substantially and developed noticeably. Based on the Leadership Style Versatility as an established psychometric test, programme directors measured the class's actual learning based on a typical 360°analysis. This includes self-evaluations, the score awarded by their bosses at work, their peers on the same level, and their subordinates or direct reports - in this case, a part-time master programme where the participants continued their learning.

The scoring in the figure is relatively easy to interpret. A positive change of +1 is significant; and students receiving scores of +2 in the figure, should be highly recommended. Not a single student was left behind and, as the stakeholders confirmed, they all grew noticeably. This is an example of the type of inclusive, transformative and effective learning experience of heartfulness in education that educators should target and measure. Given the motto that no-one should be left behind, it is important to not only focus on the easy cases, i.e. those individuals who progress almost effortlessly, but also on harder cases.

While experienced teachers and faculty members certainly hone their intuition or have hunches regarding how much progress their classes have actually made, measuring is key. It is therefore essential to bear in mind that performance measurement approaches might seem perfect on paper, but, in reality, their implementation should evolve over time. There must be protection against taking shortcuts and misinterpretations of guidelines, because such guidelines are always just a means to an end, never the end themselves.

Figure 8: An example of how to measure progress at a business master level as part of tertiary education

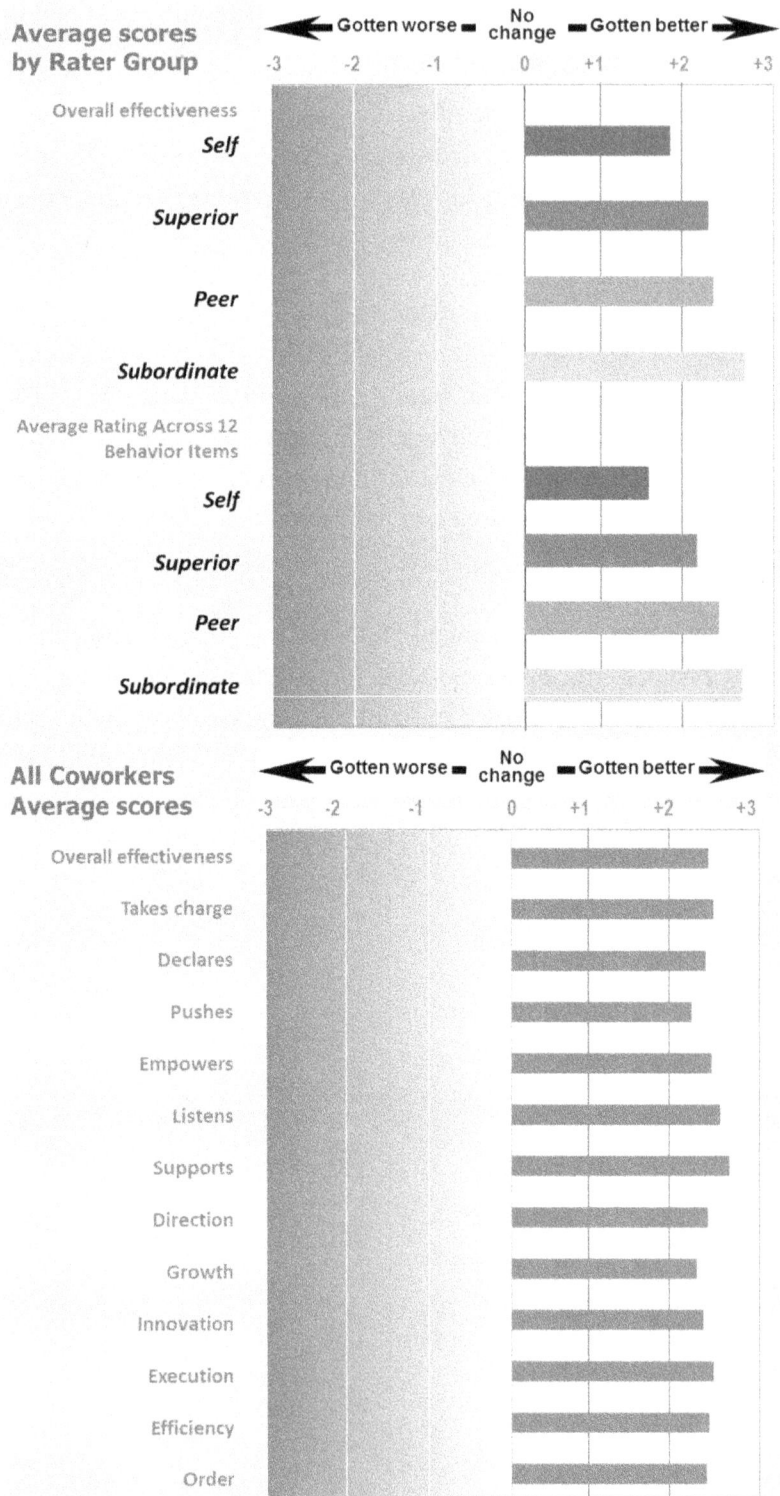

Step 6: Preparing the organisation for continuous improvement

Organisational leaders in the education sector and beyond whom I have met at training seminars, often exhibit the 'wet dog' effect, which is linked to reading inspirational books or event attendance. Often overenthusiastic, these individuals return to their organisation and risk the wet dog effect. This effect refers to a wet dog shaking off excess water and soaking those around them – not necessarily to the people's liking who are next to them. Such behaviour bears the risk of a new concept reaching an organisation prematurely, without the relevant leaders really knowing or having examined just how much readiness for change there actually is at their organisations. Heartfulness needs professional organisational development and leadership skills. It requires preparation work.

Fortunately, for aspirational heartfulness leaders, various tools create transparency. The figure below is one such tool in the form of the organisational culture circumplex model[vii], which measures an institution's culture based on four dimensions. With regard to the organisational mission, it asks: Do we know where we are going? It scrutinises the consistency of values and behaviours by asking: Does our system support us? Wanting to know whether there is involvement, it asks: Are our people aligned and engaged? Finally, when analysing transparency, it wonders: Are we listening to the stakeholders?

Measuring once or twice per year allows the heartfulness leader to know whether change should be more revolutionary or only incrementally and what to focus on to increase readiness for change. The tool likewise signals potential gaps and biases, such as an optimism bias, which is shown in the following figure. At the top, the eight organisational leaders reveal that they have a rather functional culture. The more each of the dimensions is filled out and the less empty, white space there is the better. Organisational leaders are fit for change but might overestimate what can be done within their organisation. The culture scores of the lower level staff members at the bottom of the subsequent figure tell a different story about the organisation. The 151 staff members in this sample organisation are disengaged, not sufficiently involved, teamwork is poor, the organisational goals are unclear, individuals disagree regarding the lack of consistency and are not ready for change. Change must build on the right organisational culture, which ideally fosters continuous improvement over time. It is not enough to merely have heartfulness aspirations. The aspirations have to be combined with the leadership acumen and organisational insights.

Figure 9: Organizational culture scores to indicate organisational fitness

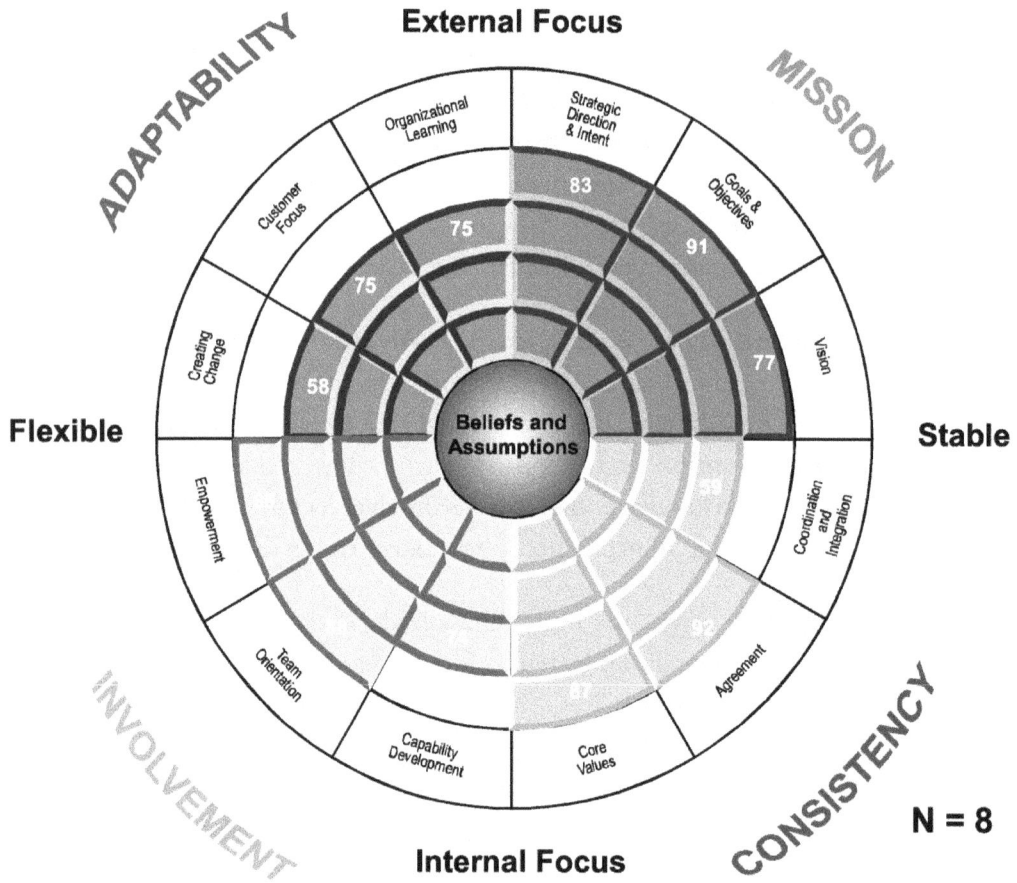

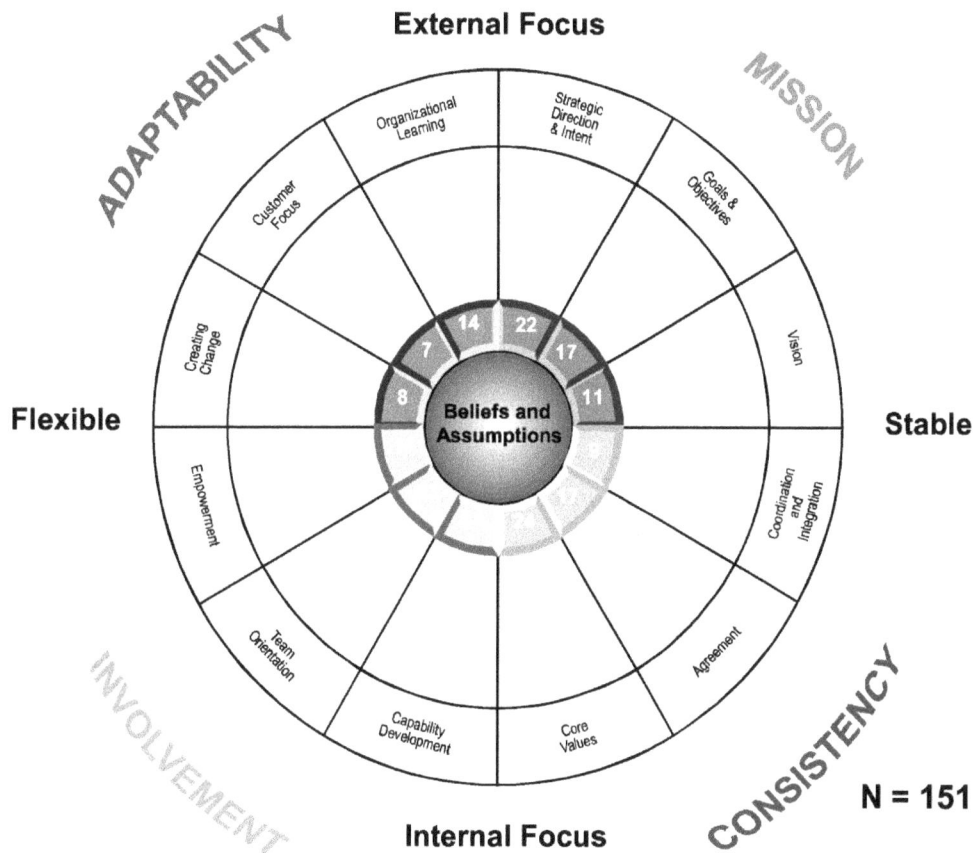

Contingent upon the organisational fitness, the functionality for further organisational change and the aspired degree of progress, heartfulness-oriented leaders should ask themselves to what extent they could move their organisation and its required skills, or how they could address the identified gaps. The wet dog effect should be avoided at cost, as it will, at best, cause a nuisance and, in the worst case, substantial frustrations. In this context, the fastest way to go slow is to go fast. Progress towards heartfulness requires preparation and an awareness of the actual change readiness in a given situation.

Step 7: Managing crises with heartfulness as the ultimate litmus test

Upholding aspirational values in times of secure budgets and a lack of smaller or bigger crises is obviously much easier than when facing a huge crisis. The Covid-19 crisis, which has been haunting educational institutions since the spring of 2020, has created totally different realities. However, does an organisation not only stick to heartfulness on sunny days, but also when conditions worsen? Organisational leaders need to clarify their priorities proactively.

During the Covid-19 crisis, many institutions either suspended their classes or used online teaching, although they often did not have the correct technology in place, nor had prepared pedagogic or andragogic solutions. The Covid-19 crisis tempted school leaders to focus on cost savings first, making their teachers responsible for the resulting complexity. Studies soon emerged that the lockdown might cause lasting psychological repercussions. Other studies suggested that the impromptu online learning destroyed 75% of the learning progress that would otherwise have been made in the regular classroom setting. Experts suggested that a segment of learners might never recover from the months of deteriorating learning – ever. Both teachers and learners' social needs were ignored when institutions tried to pragmatically recreate a minimum of learning experiences online. Parents were forced to become substitute teachers, thus neglecting their jobs at a time when job security was not a given and their employers shifted into crisis mode.

How do heartfulness-oriented leaders and teachers at educational institutions operate? They promote heartfulness even in times of adversity. They take parents' complaints seriously. In addition, they know that it is only a fairy tale that online learning is an adequate and effective solution, especially when there is no evidence to prove this, nor an emergency plan or experience of it. They remain hones and transparent. If their tuitions fees are expensive, their payment deadlines are soft instead of hard and are exempted if students experience hardship. Exchanges with peers and training become an even greater priority. They build support teams and ensure that they learn lessons for the next crisis.

3.4. Conclusions

Hirst (2020) maintained that being busy might well be a form of laziness and that lazy thinking might even be a rather indiscriminate action. He also coined the notion that those leading and managing educational institutions in today's overstimulating world should find the 'weapons of mass distraction' and neutralise them. If people feel they are too busy to embark on a journey towards quantitatively more and qualitatively better versions of heartfulness over time, the question arises whether there is a strong enough focus on what really matters. A certain type of laziness might well prevent them pausing and refocusing. This chapter and book serve as such a pause and opportunity to reflect. Are organisational priorities still spot on?

As outlined at the beginning of the chapter, educational leaders have to earn their legitimacy in terms of their place in the educational sector - not merely through their years on the job or many hours of busyness, but through focused action. This book posits that efforts towards heartfulness could allow them to gain this legitimacy.

Can there be too much heartfulness? First of all, on the whole, this chapter and book build on the assumption that, primarily, there is a need for more heartfulness. Many schools and higher education institutions are run like formal bureaucracies. This organisational concept, which Max Weber developed some 100 years ago, was supposed to ensure fairness and efficiency. However, in the meanwhile, more effective ways of organising and leading have emerged. There is a large gap to bridge before any discussion on the effects of too much heartfulness will be deemed worthwhile. Empathy is a concept closely related to heartfulness. The latter helps us gain a better understanding of the learner and all the stakeholders involved in educational institutions, such as the staff members and parents.

Waytz (2016) wonders if there are limits to empathy. According to him, it could be exhausting, a zero-sum game, because by having more empathy for one group would mean less attention, love and heartfulness for another. Preferential empathy could therefore create unfairness. Finally, too much empathy could mean that those exhibiting it might ignore ethics by overlooking loyal followers' misbehaviour and transgressions. However, Waytz (2016) overlooks that, from his perspective, the motivation to pursue empathy seems largely extrinsic, which at least partly accounts for risks' materialisation. Empathy and heartfulness should, very much like pursuing human dignity on a more abstract level, not be a means to an end, but the end in itself. Involved educational leaders should feel intrinsically motivated to make advances. Simultaneously, they ought to be aware that, as with any organisational innovation, leadership could easily derail and that success is not automatically guaranteed. As outlined in the sections above, educational leaders should have the right skills to effectively transform organisations over time. In this regard, Waytz (2016) merely warns of the derailment risks.

Regarding the question whether or not there can be too much heartfulness, we could learn from the traditional ying and yang concept or from many of its modern versions regarding organisational balance. Yin refers to the female principle in nature and yang to the male counterpart. Together, they make one aware of the integration of opposites. Organisations thrive best if their principles are in balance. Heartfulness does not equate to an imbalance. In contrast and in line with the ying and yang concept, heartfulness fosters a balance between love and discipline, between nurturing and challenging learners. This chapter builds on the insight that the heart factor might be easily lost in formal bureaucracies and has been attacked by the 'weapons of mass distraction'. There needs to be a stronger emphasis on balance and more heartfulness – always aimed at re-establish a sound balance of mind. Education is not merely about meeting budgets, making a profit, implementing a curriculum, complying with contractually agreed upon hours, or with the most vocal, active, powerful or even aggressive stakeholders. It is not about teaching either, but about enabling great, unique learning experiences and an actual education.

References

- Bolat, Y., & Bas, M. (2018). The perception of the educational philosophy in the industrial age 4.0 and the educational philosophy productivity of teacher candidates. World Journal of Education, 8(3), 149–161.

- Datar, S., Garvin, D., & Cullen, P. (2010). Rethinking the MBA: business education at a crossroads. Harvard Business School Press.

- Duff, A., & Duffy, T. (2002). Psychometric properties of Honey & Mumford's Learning Styles Questionnaire (LSQ). Personality and Individual Differences, 33(1), 147–163.

- Hirst, R. (2020). Being busy is a form of laziness, lazy thinking and indiscriminate action. Retrieved from https://www.tenfoldaustralia.com/post/being-busy-is-a-form-of-laziness-lazy-thinking-and-indiscriminate-action

- Marzano, R., & Kendall, J. (2007). The new taxonomy of educational objectives. Corwin Press.

- Phillips, J. (2003). Return on investment in training and performance improvement programs. Butterworth-Heinemann.

- Waytz, A. (2016). The limits of empathy. Harvard Business Review. https://hbr.org/2016/01/the-limits-of-empathy.

Chapter 4: What's love got to do with it? Why education needs love to be effective

Ernst von Kimakowitz

4.1. Introduction

As I am writing this article on Guru Purnima, it is dedicated to all educators that embrace or seek to gain an understanding of love as an integral part of their teaching practices. Of particular relevance to me is, that also from a Humanistic Management perspective researching, teaching or practicing Humanistic Management in a meaningful way is not possible without love. In fact, love, or when I talk to business audiences, I often label it as empathy or compassion, is one of the five key drivers that promote and empower Humanistic Management.

But how do we define love in the first place? When looking for a definition of love it becomes fast apparent that it describes strongly positive emotions or mental states that we all know yet have great difficulty to express in exactly the right words. So for the purpose of this article we can view love the same way as we view it in Humanistic Management where it describes a deep and positive emotional connection to an activity and / or the people who are carrying it out, that is free of self-interest, strategic calculus or the expectation of direct personal gains.

It is difficult at times to talk about love in a professional context but that rarely keeps us from practicing our capacity to love, regardless of whether or not we are aware of it. To name but a few examples, acts of kindness, a heightened understanding for the needs of others, a supportive and collaborative attitude, or the ability to put the achievement of a collective or of others above one's own when it serves a shared purpose, all result from, or are enhanced by love and have a profound impact on the success of an organization or activity as well as on the happiness of those who are involved, including the one demonstrating love.

In this article I am presenting five arguments on love and education, or more specifically, why love of the teacher to teach and the learner to learn is an unparalleled driver of learning outcomes. In doing so I do not want to sound naïve and am well aware that some, if not much of what I am writing here is best understood as regulative ideas in the Kantian sense (Kant, 1781). As such they represent ideals we strive for even if we are aware that we may never be able to fully achieve their realization. At least for me I know that I have failed at times on delivering what I am proposing here and will likely do so again but it does not keep me from reminding myself of the pivotal role love plays in teaching and learning and it does not keep me from wanting to inch closer to that ideal every time I teach.

The five points I will highlight in this article are: 1) Teaching and learning are two sides of the same coin. 2) A teacher can best instil a love for learning in students when having a love for teaching. 3) The teacher learner relationship is reciprocal. 4) Effective learning touches the learner beyond his or her cognitive capacity. 5) Each learner is an autonomous, dignified individual.

4.2. Teaching and learning are two sides of the same coin

Probably the most foundational of the five arguments I am presenting here to underline the critical role of love in education is that teaching and learning is very much the same thing viewed from a different angle: Teaching is always also self-learning and learning is always also self-teaching. In fact, ever since Edgar Dale (1946) has visualized learning retention under different teaching methods with his Cone of Experience often also labelled as the learning pyramid we know that teaching itself has the highest retention rate. In other words, the teacher learns most whilst listening to a lecture scores lowest so that teaching itself is the most effective way to learn. This means that learning objectives are best achieved when the teacher takes deliberate measures to create situations in which the student becomes the teacher. Doing so however requires more flexibility of the teacher, a willingness to voluntarily give up a position of power and the ability to accept the validity of positions that stand in conflict with the teachers own views and beliefs.

This is not an easy proposition, but a love of teaching enables the teacher to overcome the comfort of a position of power and put the learners' interests first. In doing so the teacher will aim to actively assume the role of the learner, being taught by her or his students while simultaneously, stimulated through this role reversal, guiding them towards achieving learning outcomes that they would not be able to attain otherwise.

4.3. A love of teaching can best instil a love of learning

As we have seen above, teaching and learning are two sides of the same coin making it a logical conclusion that, knowingly or not, a teacher that truly loves to teach is also person that loves to learn. This is no small matter for the capacity of the teacher to instil a love of learning in the student, and a love of learning is in turn a pivotal factor in a person's ability to develop and grow to live a happy and fulfilled life.

Authenticity, leading by example, being able to provide genuine examples from one's own life, providing convincing narratives on the relevance of learning and all the non-verbal communication that comes with talking about something one loves to do are transferred to the learner by teachers that love to teach. If successful, the pattern of a virtuous circle will emerge where the leaner is inspired to study more by a teacher that loves to teach and will acquire new knowledge that is empowering to the learner and creates a desire to learn more.

"If students come to feel a capacity within themselves which they had not felt or were fully aware of before, then they are on the way to a love of learning. This in turn leads to a willingness to continue to learn, to reflect, and to develop throughout one's life" (Nillsen, 2004, p. 16) Being empowered to do something one was previously excluded from, purely by learning and acquiring new knowledge is profoundly liberating and boosts our confidence. We love the empowering effect of knowledge and with it a strong foundation is being laid for developing a love of learning.

4.4. The teacher learner relationship is reciprocal

From school children to senior executives, the teacher student relationship is reciprocal as in that the teacher always also learns from the learner and not only vice versa. Consequently, teaching and learning is not only the different side of the same coin in an auto-reflexive understanding but it is reciprocal as the roles of who is teacher and who is learner are interchanging throughout learning situations.

"Learning and teaching are active processes occurring simultaneously on a continual basis. Within this framework, the learner and the teacher are reliant on each other. Understanding the intricacies of this linkage enhances the teacher's effectiveness in enabling learners to achieve their full potential" (Forrest, 2004, p. 64) Therefore in a teaching set-up one needs to recognize that meaningful learning is based meeting students at eye level and only compassion, empathy, a love for teaching, for learning and for the learner can ensure we meet students at eye level.

Regardless of how the teacher's achievements, status, power or age may differ from those of the student in an educative setting, when teacher and learner are together a genuinely reciprocal relationship can deliver heightened learning outcomes. It prevents the teacher from falling for temptations to use hierarchical positions or the coercive power of grading and evaluating student deliverables to behave in ways that are adversely affecting learning. This capacity of a teacher to meet students at eye level is strongly related to love as it is the deep emotional connection to the activity of teaching itself that enables a teacher to remove him- or herself from the formal position held and immerse in a joint learning experience with students.

4.5. Effective teaching touches the learner

To be effective in teaching the learner needs to be touched more holistically than just in her or his cognitive capacity. The proverbial addressing of the head, heart and hands is crucial to consolidate learning experiences. "The holistic learning approach, which embraces the affective, psychomotor and cognitive domains in equal measure […] is oriented towards satisfying individual's cognitive, affective and practical interests, which is also the objective of contemporary education" (Gazibara, 2013, p. 56)

We can take a look at the type of feedback received in course evaluations through which higher education institutions aim to improve learning outcomes. Student feedbacks such as: "I felt really inspired by this course", "the teacher made me want to learn more about the subject matter", "This course has made an impact on my career aspirations", "I felt I was in charge of my own learning experience" or "I had the opportunity to develop different skills in this course that are relevant for my future" are all highly desirable while they cannot be realized when teaching is only focused on the cognitive capacity of the learner.

To be effective in teaching, the teacher must touch students much more deeply than addressing only their cognitive capacity and a love of teaching plays a dual role here. It inherently endorses the affective domain while it encourages the teacher to seek balance in addressing the head, heart and hands of the learner.

4.6. Each learner is an autonomous, dignified individual

We do not like all people the same, throughout our lives we meet people with whom "we click" or with whom "the chemistry is right" and we meet those where this is not happening. These need not be adversaries in fact sometimes we click with adversaries and have nothing to share with allies but be this as it may, educators need a love of teaching to overcome interpersonal preferences in the teacher learner relationship. Love protects the teacher learner relationship from being tainted by questions of sympathy so that every learner receives the same opportunity to learn and that the teacher is aiming to cater as best as he or she can, to individual learning needs and learning goals.

This requires on one hand to view each student as a dignified individual that shall not be limited in her or his capacity to lead a self-determined life by partialities of the teacher. And, on the other hand it requires to respect the autonomy of each learner in the way as Phil Benson (2000) defined it in his article titled Autonomy as a learners' and teachers' right where he wrote that "Autonomy is a recognition of the rights of learners within educational systems" (p. 111) which in turn is closely linked to respecting the learners dignity. Learners have a right to choose their learning goals without being subjected to the will of others. This of course should not impede the teacher from guiding the learner and encouraging self-reflection on learning goals, but subsequent learner choices are to be respected as decisions made by an autonomous, dignified individual. Again, it is the love of teaching, learning and the learner that enhances learning outcomes. In this fifth dimension of the relevance of love in education I am presenting in this article, love encourages the teacher to respect learner autonomy when formulating learning goals and inspires the teacher to support the student in achieving them.

4.7. Concluding remarks on love and education

This article has presented five dimensions on the relevance of love of teaching, learning and the learner aiming to sketch out and underline the pivotal role love has in achieving learning outcomes. In *Pedagogy of the Oppressed*, first published in 1968, Paulo Freire (2000) equated learning relationships with love. Based on our inherent human capacity and desire to learn about the complexities of our world and share the experiences we make in it, a teacher is always also a learner and a learner always also a teacher. A love of teaching heightens our awareness of this interplay and provides an anchor to reflect on the role of education and ways to enhance learning outcomes by promoting a love of learning. Love enables the teacher and the learner to meet at eye level, creating holistic learning experiences that overcome a singular focus on our cognitive capacity and respect the learner as an autonomous dignified individual. For education to unfold its uniquely liberating effect and enhance our ability to live self-determined lives, a love of teaching, learning and the learner is an unparalleled driver that ought to be an integral part of how we educate.

References

- Benson, P. (2000). Autonomy as a learners' and teachers' right. In B. Sinclair, I. McGrath & T. Lamb (eds.), Learner autonomy, teacher autonomy (pp. 111–117). Longman.

- Dale, E. (1946). Audio-visual methods in teaching. Dryden Press.

- Freire, P. (2000). Pedagogy of the oppressed. Continuum.

- Gazibara, S. (2013). Head, heart and hands learning - A challenge for contemporary education. Journal of Education Culture and Society, 1, 71–82.

- Forrest, S. (2004). Learning and teaching: The reciprocal link. The Journal of Continuing Education in Nursing, 35(2), 74–79.

- Kant, I. (1791). Kritik der reinen Vernunft. ZVAB.

- Nillsen, R. (2004). Can the love of learning be taught? Journal of University Teaching & Learning Practice, 1(1), 65-79.

Chapter 5: The transformative leader as spiritual behavioural strategist: Insights from Indian wisdom for developing heartful leadership in education

Anand Joshi

5.1. Introduction

Holistic Transformational change in Educational Institution is possible with human factors and connectedness, as the institution is human centric by its' fundamental nature. Faculty members, who are the main change agents in the knowledge creation and dissemination process, are human beings with strong intellectual and emotional traits. The whole idea of an an academic institution is to ensure the holistic and balanced growth of a person. The transformational leadership can be best achieved through human connectedness and emotional intelligence.

The Present day's academic leaders, armed with yesterday's academic protocols, are frequently found to be ill-equipped to deal with the challenges. Therefore, what are the new standards by which we should judge leadership? What is a model of leadership that fits into this age of disruption? It is the responsibility of leaders to hone these intelligences and cultivate cognitive complexity. Each of these intelligences is essential; *it is their artful combination that generates the real power of smart leadership.*

Among the Indian ancient writings, it is said that, *"Vedas are the earliest known oral books"*. The 'Gurus' emphasized on the importance of humans to realize their humility, spiritual insights and social behaviour in the infinite universe before embarking on the long journey of learning. When the system of education was eventually institutionalized, the focus switched to intellectual quotient from that of emotional intelligence and there started the decline of human connectedness. It is fundamental to establish different dimensions to leadership in academic institutions. In the next section of the chapter, we will explore the different leadership approaches, which are relevant for fostering heartful wisdom development in academic institutions.

5.2. Wisdom leadership for wisdom development

There are different sources of the leadership which drive or shape the processes in the given contexts.

Here ten such leadership dimensions are suggested which can complement each other to drive wisdom leadership for wisdom development.

a. Leadership by Knowledge Dissemination through "Human Library" or "Oral Books"

In line with 'Oral Books' in ancient times, the concept of *"Human Library or living library"* is a concept of "learning through other person or the interface between learned and learner". The ancient Gurukul system is a classic example of teaching through oral books. The knowledge disseminated from person to person through several generations and was never converted into textual forms. The movement of Human Library started in Denmark in 2000 and spread across 80 countries. The Living Library or Human Library is a unique event that brings together people who have special interests, beliefs or experiences to speak with people from different backgrounds and share their personal stories. The Human library in institutions can be in the following forms:

i.   The learned elderly with a group of people.

ii. Ideation, not content based, not a textual discussion with experienced person Ideas is converted into a research or a business model.

iii. Framework based discussion, where questions are asked of practical intelligence on the topic. The questions are appreciated, analysed and answered.

iv. Pages are replaced with living books wherein practical wisdom is discussed on a conceptual theory.

v.   In a library, students can borrow some time with a person for an hour or so instead of a book.

vi. People are open books who need wisdom, to analyse information and to apply in practical issues, also who seek wisdom with an experientially learned person. *Chandogya Upanishad says that the* reader of a text is the owner of *"apara vidya"* and will not gain wisdom till he applies it!

In a university, it can be a mandatory credit course on selected topics or framework to the students. The institution must identify five to ten seniors with Experiential learning as "human books "in selected topics and students will be evaluated based on a report on the analysis of discussion.

b. Leadership with "EQ" Vs "IQ"

World Economic Forum report says "The emotional intelligence first appeared to the masses, people with average IQs outperform those with the highest IQs 70% of the time. This anomaly threw a massive wrench into what many people had always assumed was the sole source of success—IQ.

Decades of research now point to emotional intelligence as the critical factor that sets star performers apart from the rest of the pack"

Emotional intelligence is the "trait" and quite intangible in human being. It affects how a leader manages behaviour, navigates social complexities, and makes personal decisions that achieve positive results. Emotional intelligence is made up of four core skills that pair up under two primary competencies: Personal competence and Social competence.

c. Leadership in Science and Art of Learning

The Indian Ancient literature refers to the science of learning "*Jnana*" as two components viz., "*Paroksha vidya*" and "*Aparoksha Vidya*". The paroksha vidya refers to the Institutional learning where in the students used to stay with Guru for knowledge and also to learn life skills i.e.," Jeevana Vidya". In the context of current institutionalised education system, Paroksha Vidya is Institutional learning which is classroom driven and examination oriented. Aparoksha Vidya is knowledge driven, application oriented experiential learning. It's also called Collaborative learning through viz., seminars, conferences, group internship, group projects. These are some beyond classroom learning and beyond campus learnings. Aparoksha vidya helps in developing practical intelligence, power of thinking and power of expression. The leader should drive the system of learning in an institution.

d. Thought Leadership

An academic institution is a totally human centric knowledge industry. It is a treasure of intellectual capital, with the quality of faculty and the right mix of students. The thought leader is one who has a flow of positive thoughts. The thoughts are peaceful, purposeful, powerful and are not pointless! The thought leader is one who does not find fault with others and has no place for jealousy, hatred and one-upmanship. These are typical positive behavioural traits of an individual.

The term "Thought leader" is used in modern times, to add flavour to a person or a leader! In accordance with Bhagawad Gita, the *Rajyogi* is one who obtains a non-dualistic state of consciousness in which the mind becomes still though the person remains conscious. It helps to attain the power of concentration, increase the memory power and reduces the wastage of energy. The role of a thought leader is to create idea/knowledge and disseminate it.

e. Leadership by Democratisation of Knowledge

With increase in the power of technology and tools for technology enabled learning, the Institutions are no longer the power centres of knowledge. The role of teachers, the academic leader and institutional leader has changed to bring intellectual leadership and is not just dissemination of bundle of knowledge and awarding grades.

The students learn in the form of self-learning, peer learning or experiential learning as no two persons process the same information in the same way. The ability of the leader to understand the learning ability of the students. This will bring the best out of them, than placing all students in one bracket.

f. *Leadership with Contextual intelligence and Inclusive Orientation*

There is a need for ongoing mechanisms in Institutions to achieve clarity both about their current situation as well as their desired outcomes. It can be assessed with divergent perspectives, exercising intuition in appropriate measure, perceiving weak signals, and conducting mental rehearsals for unimaginable outcomes. These are all approaches to cultivating contextual intelligence. Context intelligence must be supported by inclusive workplace.

g. *Leadership with integrity and sustained core values*

All journeys express a purpose that is shaped by a particular set of values. Strategy (what we must do) is how we realize our mission (what we seek to achieve) which in turn reflects our purpose (why we're in business) which is based on our values (our enduring beliefs.)

The application of "Dharma" is relevance of ancient wisdom to modern times. The term "Dharma" according to ancient literature is "Human conduct indicated in the form of ethical lifestyle that represents ideal for humanity". In fact, the Human science supports this version. Dharma is duties and responsibilities towards Family, Fraternity, Society and the most important is "self-conduct". This is what is considered in management quotes as Leadership by Example.

h. *Leadership based on Impact Social Innovation*

Social and emotional intelligence expresses our values in terms of how we interact with and influence others. We connect through our empathy and compassion - our ability to put ourselves into the shoes of another. The concept of simple living of a person is a model of sustained personal economy. In fact, the Upanishad says space, air, water, fire and earth are interconnected it's our dharma to protect them as "panchamahabhtas".

i. *Leadership by generative intelligence*

The ability to produce new ideas and realize value from them is the engine that provides the "how" of journey to a desired future. Generative intelligence brings a fundamental leadership question. Generative intelligence amplifies the power of ideas. It's also called Intellectual leadership wherein the leader is responsible to generate new knowledge, identify the market trend and also be relevant to the society and Industry.

j. *Leadership by Technology & Digital intelligence*

Leaders must be able to understand, make use of and amplify the power of rapidly emerging technologies and their impact. This is a new set of literacies that apply not only to business models but to organizations and how they function.

5.3. Transformative to spiritual leadership: The leader as a behavioural strategist

Transformative leadership can be viewed as an ability to create and drive a meaningful roadmap will motivate people to act and align their efforts. Such a roadmap comes alive with clear, credible communication, compelling narratives and evangelism by credible leaders that drives a sense of urgency.

The Indian philosophy deals with nature of human mind. It endeavours to understand that all comes with bounds of human experience based on religious, spiritual and scientific beliefs. The Bhagwad Gita is the oldest literature on the philosophy of life which is relevant event today. The science of spirituality has a direct interface with human science with the following:

- Development of competence to live

- Define the human conduct

- Strong social and fraternity connectivity

- Strong connectivity with family and friends

- Emotional connectivity with family and friends

- Positive Professional behaviour

- Positive Social behaviour

In conclusion, the academic institutions today are considered as learning organisations. Leading an institution with a climate conducive to learning with psychological safety, particularly in the post era of covid -19 is important. As referred in the 'Eesavaasya Upanishad" the institution should focus on both scientific knowledge and spiritual knowledge. Further the leader should have Human judgement. As an entity, the leader should drive the decision making with 'mind and metrics'

The role of education has a direct impact on the human society. It's also called "Jeevana Vidya". The conduct of human being is based on education i.e., "Sanskara" Literacy is increasing and inhuman behaviour is increasing. There is also fear among noble people of inhuman behaviour of people which is increasing. It's the responsibility of the leader to nurture a team which have not only academic brilliance but also have positive behavioural traits. The leader should ensure positive personality dimensions in moral, ethical, emotional, behavioural, social and cultural moulding.

5.4. Conclusions

Heartfulness is an approach, quality, outcome as well as the process. In context of the academic leadership, heartfulness can be achieved when we integrate the different dimensions of knowledge creation and dissemination with the different determinants of heartful leadership. This chapter provides 10 such leadership approaches which an academic leader can integrate in order to ensure greater impact. These approaches are neither prescriptive nor mutually exclusive and, therefore, as per the contextual requirements, one can always tailor one's leadership in the given context and scenario.

Chapter 6: An academic entrepreneur's perspective on developing heartful leadership

Umesh Mukhi and Saurabh Saha

6.1. Introduction

One of the direct outcomes of the COVID-19 pandemic across the globe is the widespread discussion within civil society about developing the resilience and empathy for a wide variety of stakeholders we directly or indirectly depend upon. While it is easier to bring in discussion about such topics through an article or a social media post, it is difficult to practice. It is so because, for decades the society has churned itself around the neoliberal approach which has devalorized the human ability to solidarize with fellow peers. In our experience it is rare to see educational institutions and corporations making a conscious effort to integrate empathy in their mission statements. As a result, we see a plethora of graduates and working professionals who are creating a homogenized society devaluing the power of empathy which has proved to be an excellent trait for developing leadership capabilities in the recent past. The uniqueness of the chapter lies in how the authors realized the power of empathy via leadership of Abraham Lincoln through Doris Kearn Goodwin's classic book 'Team of Rivals'. The authors who come from seemingly different backgrounds share their experiences from the technology and the education sector on how they plan to fill this inordinate gap by deploying certain tools in their practice to develop" Heartful Leadership". They conclude by outlining how academics and managers can benefit from Heartful Leadership.

6.2. The technology perspective

There has been a lot of discussion in the civic society around empathy. Professor Brene Brown has been highly instrumental in popularizing empathy as a trait. She has through her books and lectures clearly distinguished between empathy and its doppelganger sympathy. Earlier most people would assume sympathy to be empathy but today things are different. Empathy is the quality of being able to feel someone's pain and say or do things to comfort the person. It's a rare ability because quite a few humans can do that. For empathy to happen, one should have had similar traumatic experiences and should have felt the pain required to relate to someone else's trauma and pain. As most psychologists articulate, every traumatic event leaves a scar in life. One has to carry the burden throughout their life. Only through empathy can the healing take place. Unfortunately, society has been quite late in understanding the significance of empathy. For a long time, people thought that just by saying nice things to a person going through a crisis, might help make things easier for her. Only in the 21st century, we have realized that empathy is an altogether different ball game.

Doris Kearn Goodwin's book 'Team of Rivals' is a masterpiece especially in the context of empathy as a trait. It's a beautifully written account of the events that led President Lincoln to choose his cabinet from a pool of people who in real life were ideological contenders of Lincoln. New York senator William Seward, Ohio Governor Salmon Chase and Missouri's distinguished statesman Edward Bates were political rivals of Lincoln before he was nominated by the Republic Party and won the primaries in 1860. Soon after getting elected as the President of the United States of America, Lincoln in a surprising turn of events invites Seward, Chase and Bates to become a part of his cabinet. Seward assumes the role of the Secretary of State, Chase that of the Secretary of Treasury and Bates becomes the United States Attorney General. Together they all made some historically significant moves that shaped America over the next 100 years or so. It was during Lincoln's time as the President of the United States of America, that slavery was abolished, right after the civil war, when the 13th Amendment was written to strike off slavery from the books forever. This is a shining example of one of the best cabinets the world has ever seen, where four brilliant minds worked together to do nation building effectively keeping aside their ideological differences.

What sets this book from a host of other books is the singular fact that it shows Lincoln's life in an altogether different light. It shows Lincoln as a normal person growing up to become a lawyer. What sets Lincoln apart from his contemporaries is the fact that as a child growing up, he witnessed so many deaths in front of him of people he really loved. This continued across his life as he by a twist of fate kept on losing people, he was fond of. The amount of losses Lincoln suffered during his lifetime could have easily driven a normal person to insanity, but Lincoln held on. It's because of these untimely losses that Lincoln developed a superlative sense of empathy. He could relate to the pain suffered by people. He could talk to them like they were his friends. He could comfort people in distress by his words and his deeds. This ingenious ability to empathize with other people made Lincoln a popular figure even as a lawyer before he became the President of America. It was his empathy levels that made him abolish slavery as he could experience the ghastly treatment meted out to slaves. I have used 'Team of Rivals' as a reference to demonstrate how empathy plays out in the technology world.

I have spent close to two decades in the technology world in various roles across many geographies. One thing that I have learnt is that technological growth has been the sole reason behind the growth of human civilization. It has helped make things easier for humans. It has achieved things thought to be impossible five decades back. But it took the technology industry a royal amount of time before it made this seemingly impossible jump. The biggest obstacle it has had to face was religious persecution. Giordino Bruno, Galileo Galilei and Nicolaus Copernicus had to face the wrath of the church for coming up with scientific theories that defied what the church was preaching. So, it wasn't an easy path for technologists born on the wrong side of history. Gradually civilizations started accepting technology as they understood how it helps reduce human effort and increase productivity. From then till now, we have managed to come a long way. But what is surprising is that till a few decades back, the technology industry did not understand the semantics of sentience. It had no clue about empathy. It was busy building technology to solve human needs defined by Abraham Maslow in his seminal Pyramid of Needs model.

What really changed and how did empathy become an integral part of every product manager's playbook? We'd have to go back a little to when Steve Jobs launched Apple 2 and subsequently iPhone, iPad and iPods. Steve jobs was a design connoisseur, but he understood customer experience quite well. He knew that it always starts backwards from customer experience and moves down to technology eventually. Steve Jobs knew that one needs to build technology for humans not the other way around. He understood that the only way to win the race is to provide superlative customer experience that would be used and appreciated by customers over and over again. In fact, Jonathan Ive, who was a Steve Jobs aficionado, in one of his quotes says that he was more than ready to humanize technology. If one looks at every element of an Apple product, one would find that it is extremely simple to use even for a layman. The products are designed keeping the customer in mind.

Another company that comes to mind when talking about customer empathy is Zappos. Tony Hseih, the founder of Zappos, like Steve Jobs, understood the value of customer experience quite early on. He codified customer experience as a 'Wow experience' that every Zappos customer should have and keep coming back for more. Everything at Zappos was created around customer happiness. Their firm belief was that customers need to feel special when they order shoes from Zappos and the experience should make them feel so elated that they end up coming back for more. Their firm belief in customer happiness worked wonders for Zappos. It was their laser sharp focus on customer happiness that caught the eye of Amazon, another customer centric company and eventually Amazon acquired Zappos and the rest as they say is history.

What the technology industry has now understood is that customer happiness lies at the forefront of their business and empathy has a powerful role to play in that. It has also understood an unconscious bias called the 'empathy gap' which a large number of techies suffer from. 'Empathy Gap' is defined as a bias in which a person from one background cannot empathize with another from an entirely different background. If you look at the systems that were designed 3 decades back and then compare them to the systems that are built now, you'd see a huge difference in the way today's systems are shaped to create a blissful user experience. Matter of fact one of the reasons 'design thinking' became an integral part of every product manager's toolkit is to enable product teams to understand more about the customer to empathize with her. Today a lot of efforts are being put to understand more and more about the customer. Some of the most successful emerging technologies that have helped understand deeply about customers would be artificial intelligence, data science, machine learning and deep learning. Today we gather behavioral data, ethnographic data and apply game theory to understand more about customers. But at the crux of everything lies human empathy. Most of the emerging technology is used to understand more about customer groups and the problems they face. It is then the company puts in a lot of efforts around doing focus groups or user interviews or surveys or pilots.

Today human empathy has become the core of every business. Most tech businesses have started because the founders themselves faced an issue and then found others facing the same issue. Brian Chesky faced a genuine issue when he found that it was almost next to impossible to find an affordable place to stay in a city. That led Chesky to start AirBnB to help people stay in different cities at affordable prices in houses that were vacant as the owner was in a different place. It led to a win-win situation for all and helped AirBnB become a unicorn. Hard to see at first but empathy actually helped AirBnB create an industry out of nowhere.

Having said all that in favor of customer empathy, it's pertinent to know that empathy has to exist for all the stakeholders in a corporate utopia. Vineet Nayar the ex-CEO of HCL wrote a book a long time back called 'Employees First Customers Second'. Nayar specified that in a bid to please customers sometimes organizations tend to shift their attention away from employees. The corresponding empathy deficit can have a devastating effect on the health of the organization. It's quite evident in the delivery and over time will result in large deficits in productivity unless management acknowledges it.

The idea is to create a circle of empathy that has the power to create products that can leave an indelible impression in the minds of users. The technology industry is getting there but it will happen over several iteration cycles. We have seen the first version of any product just trying to solve a need devoid of any kind of empathy and then the subsequent versions come up with more empathy laden feature sets that empathize with the customers. We have also seen the emergence of cross disciplinary teams in the technology industry where humanities students are seated with engineers, designers, data scientists and the likes to create products and feature sets that can start with customer empathy at its core. It seems the empathy revolution has just started for the technology industry, but we still have a long way to go.

6.3. The business school perspective: Insights from teaching

As my colleague just highlighted the importance of Empathy from his experience within the industry, my dilemma as a business school professor is altogether different. I begin by thinking, how can I curate the pedagogical experience so that my students can develop Empathy? This is even a greater challenge when it comes to executive education where executives spend a large amount of time in the industry and weekends on the education. If I have to do math, it is clearly visible that they will be in my course on Saturday for 2 hours and 30minutes for 10 sessions. Considering this, I have 22hours and 30mins to develop these skills centred around Empathy through whatsoever tools I have in my pedagogical kit. Thus, inspired from the Team of Rivals I decided to develop an elective course titled "Sustainable Leadership: Lessons from The Lives of Lincoln and Mandela" taught at FGV EAESP, Brazil. This leadership elective had 7 students and was based on experimental pedagogy where executives (students now onwards) and I as a faculty engaged in creating a reflective space to develop empathy and inspiration, principally based on the lives of President Lincoln and Nelson Mandela. Specifically, for this course, I took a critical stance of understanding and discussing Leadership through classical theories and organization centric case studies. I decided to oppose Leadership frameworks which oversimply leadership behaviours in linear fashion. On the contrary, I chose to emphasize that each student has to develop their own sense of relativity with Lincoln or Mandela and develop their individualized inspirational experience to develop Leadership ability. The table below outlines the details about the elective.

Table 2: Options for curriculum development

Curriculum	
a) Introduction to Lincoln and Mandela	Stimulation
b) Watching documentary on Lincoln and Mandela	
c) Assignment to read biography or autobiography of these leaders	Reflection
d) Analysis of speeches and letters of these leaders	
e) Speech and letter writing exercise	Action
f) Group presentations and article writing exercise	

Let us first begin by detailing each element which forms the crux of the elective. The curriculum is based on the Lives of Lincoln and Mandela, the reason behind this choosing this type of curriculum and elective is three-fold. Firstly, these students are Brazilian executives, they could relate the story of leaders specifically with discrimination and slavery which has been the part of the history of Brazil. Secondly, I chose to offer a differential perspective of leaders who are not from the business sector but the ones who have made large scale transformation at societal level. Thirdly, I found that it is easier to access the story of these leaders, in case of Lincoln, its biography The Team of Rivals and in case of Mandela, its autobiography: The Long Walk to Freedom. These resources supply very enriching and fine-grained analysis of their life. As it is shown in the table above below, the curriculum is divided into three parts which are stimulation, reflection and action.

a. Stimulation Part (a, b)

In this introductory part, I introduced the class by highlighting the lives of Lincoln & Mandela. I also emphasized that each student must engage in reflective experience to inspire themselves from the story of these leaders. To support this, I did short quizzes with the facts which aroused the attention of students, these were further supplemented by the 1-hour documentary movie on each leader. Showcasing the documentary helped in establishing the base level of the class so that everyone had established the basis and generic understanding about the overview of their lives and the cause for which these leaders strived.

b. Reflection Part (c, d)

After stimulating students with the story of these leaders, I asked them to choose 1 leader, either Lincoln or Mandela based on how they sense their inspiration-based on the mission and values of the leader. Hereafter, they were given the task of reading the book related to the specific leader throughout the course. The reflection is interesting because it demands continuous reading throughout the course and is not limited to class hours, since these are long books students are asked to read it throughout the course. Doing so helps them to establish individual rapport with these leaders, through which they start developing the sense of connection with them.

When these students are in class, I further supplemented the reading by showcasing specific cases highlighting the leadership skills of these leaders. For example, I shared the letters and speeches written by President Lincoln. We also watched the interview given by Mandela. Since these materials are not available in the books, they helped in supplementing the student's understanding on how these leaders used their empathy and diplomatic skills to make a significant impact. Based on this, I developed a challenge for students which is discussed in the next part.

c. Action part (e, f)

This part is related to how students can put into practice certain skills they learnt from the leaders, specifically speech and letter writing. The whole idea behind drafting the speech and letter is to engage in the process of creating a convincing and arguable content. To do so, I specifically allotted speech topics to each student while I gave them a liberty to choose the topic of letter writing. The speech topics were also relevant in nature such as Tax on Sugar Drinks, Importance of Music in Education, raising minimum wages, Challenges of Democracy for the very reason that my students were executives, they should and will have to eventually engage in real pertinent issues. Furthermore, I gave them some tips on speech writing and structure which we saw in Lincoln's and Mandela's speech. Students were now given a specific time period (2 weeks) over which they will prepare, revise and present their speech.

Finally, when they presented the speech and letters in the class, we had a very stimulating discussion and feedback session within the group. This was the most important session because each student's speech displayed the rigor and reflected on how they had engaged in drafting the speech and delivery process. It affected the class in such a way that the fellow students were inspired from each other's presentation.

Finally, the last part of the course also includes two exercises, one is group presentation and other is article writing. In group presentation, students are divided in two groups based on leaders they chose, Lincoln and Mandela respectively. These groups then have to make a collective inquiry, reflect on their individual transformational process and thereby make a presentation about how they were inspired by the life of the chosen leader. They must ponder on what episode do they think was most important, what skills do they learn from this leader and how did it change their beliefs.

In the article writing exercise, I asked them to write an article on what leadership lessons we can learn from Lincoln or Mandela and publish it on LinkedIn. The idea however to write an article is to engage them in their thought process about what they can share with the community, that they need to be aware about their target readers and that they need to give some practical tips to executives in their network who would eventually read their article.

It is obvious that for the purpose of this chapter, the curriculum is presented in the linear fashion. However, as the class proceeded, I had to sense the direction of the class and adapt the content. It is the whole class experience which makes it an engaging experience. For example, I recall that one of the students had already completed the book on Lincoln however others were yet to start reading. This particular incident stimulated other students that they cannot escape the excuses related to time management specifically when it comes to reading a few pages of the book every day.

Furthermore, my role as a faculty was as a facilitator, it is the learning space which was created in each session that had a significant impact on us. I observed that with each and every class there was a stronger cohesion, binding within the group and their ability to give feedback, as if the group had developed the empathy and the spirit of collective intelligence to reflect on important issues such as inequality discrimination and racism. In fact, certain students also recalled that they were able to apply certain skills immediately in their professional lives. For example, they used to think twice before writing an email, they used to think about the structure and the words used in their email, they had developed empathy and emotional intelligence in giving feedback to their colleagues. These are some practical takeaways which are very at once visible for me during class discussions. The student feedback outline below highlights that he was able to find safe space to go back to deep reading which is now a luxury. As we are living in the digital age, we are bound to read more articles, access more information but we are not engaging in an introspective experience.

I really liked it. As I've said, it learnt more about leadership than the leadership mandatory classes. And I've learned about writing (speeches and my thesis), learned to love reading books again (3 books – since I started my master classes and I had stopped reading articles). Amilton Cabral Jr.

6.4. Concluding thoughts: Takeaways for managers and academics

The insights around empathy in the context of business school, relates to the gap we highlighted earlier. If we were to instil empathy as an integral part of our moral fiber, then empathy needs to be taught in schools and colleges like other subjects of equivalent importance. Today most technologists who became a part of the workforce barely have time to realize that everything that they are building is for a human consumer on the other end of the spectrum. As the technology industry is becoming more aware of the nuances around empathy, fields like human centric design are emerging. The overarching idea is to use technology to solve all the problems people have. But for that to happen, technologists need to be deeply empathetic to the needs of their customers. As Clay Christensen mentions in his seminal book 'Competing Against Luck', technologists today need to be extremely receptive about how effective their solutions are in the context of getting a job done for their respective customers. Teddy Levitt in one of his famous quotes said, **"People don't want to buy quarter inch drill. They want a quarter inch hole"**. Unfortunately, most technology companies two decades back thought otherwise. The lingering perception was that keeping production high and then using an effective sales arm to push the products to the market could help the company achieve scale. Surprisingly it worked for companies like Ford, DEC, Kodak and a host of other companies till they suffered due to obsolescence. What became evident soon enough was that the customer is the most important part of the value chain. Unless efforts are put to empathize with the customers and understand more about their problems, most companies would not survive the test of time.

However, we have evolved since then. More and more companies are focusing on the customer angle and tech companies are no exception. The emergence of customer success teams in companies is a positive signal that a lot of companies are taking it seriously. Today, every inbound and outbound call are monitored to understand how effective the call was qualitatively. The new age has also unleashed a host of companies that have drifted from the earlier ideological stance of checking growth through supply side metrics. Some of the 21st century technology companies are using demand side metrics to understand more about customer happiness. Frameworks like NPS (Net Promoter Score), CSAT (Customer Satisfaction) and CES (Customer Effort Survey) are being used to understand more and more about customer happiness. Companies are increasingly focusing on achieving customer happiness at both psychological and biological levels. From a monopolistic ecosystem we are moving towards a more vibrant democratic one where customers have the say. Free market economy as envisioned by Adam Smith is a perfect model of how customers get the best products or services. It promotes empathy and makes it an extremely competitive game for technology companies to come up with the best products or services for the customers or there is always a danger of losing customers to a competitor with better services. It keeps technology companies on their toes.

The interesting part about teaching executives is that there is a lot of collective learning and action going on in parallel as the course moves along. Often the student would immediately implement course learning during their working week and will share experience within the class during the course on weekends. This is not the case with master's students who are engaged solely in studying throughout the year. Executive education thus has the potential to create continuous impact and fill the empathy gap because of the less time span required to apply the concepts. Experimental pedagogy experience is an opportunity to nourish the knowledge of the faculty and the students so that they can co-create knowledge and solutions together.

The aim of the chapter is to outline how Empathy can become as essential factor to instil the notion of "Heartful Leadership". By sharing our experiences, we have tried to create a convergence of perspectives which can help academia and executives to engage in experimental pedagogy which is simple but requires sincere efforts. Indeed, we acknowledge that our insights are limited and may be biased through our expectations, experiences and worldviews. The example highlighted of education is too specific and the views shared about the industry may be sector specific. We thus hope that both academics and executives can engage in creative discussions and brainstorming to curate enhanced learning experiences for developing leadership with heartfulness.

References

- Goodwin, D. (2009). Team of rivals: The political genius of Abraham Lincoln. Penguin.

- Mandela, N. (2013). Long walk to freedom. Hachette.

Chapter 7: Being more humane - A heartfulness approach in educational transformation

Deepti Sharma

7.1. Introduction

Man is human due to the humanity lying within. Adopting a non-spiritual perspective to prepare for a broader debate, evolution of human began from apes of different categories where there was struggle for survival. With time taking pace, the animals evolved as humans. The humans then began to use mind as well as heart for the welfare of others. The human evolution saw the emergence of word "Dharma" which came from Sanskrit word "dhri" which means "to sustain". There was Sanatana dharma which was aimed at performing duties according to one's spiritual identity as atman. Sanatan dharma was associated with Hinduism where the life was designed to ensure continuity of humanity on earth. The essence was to have more humanity aspect for other people to have holistic development of all humans. This has formed the base for various area in further development including education system. The Dharma things were taken very seriously and inculcated on that education system prevailed at that time. People uses to devote their best for transferring knowledge and skills for the development of others. Education system was base for creating a better society for living. Even today education system is of vital importance but there has been a gradual drift in aim and pedagogy related to education. Today scenario witnesses more urge for money and materialistic things in people. Sustainability has again created a competition among people which has prompted people for taking even wrong ways to achieve them. We can further understand how the system has gradually changed from ancient to modern and to current scenario.

7.2. Evolution of Indian education system from ancient to modern

Indian education history revels enrich culture for promoting and imbibing knowledge. The country has remarkable history in education which began around 8th century BCE where renowned university like Nalanda etc flourished. The aim of education in that era was majorly for enriching knowledge base for making people intellect so that they can contribute for the benefits of others and for the earth. The dedication of teachers at that point of time was remarkable. Most of the education was oral. The Indian Education System was well organised and meticulous. The prevalent process at that time was in form of "Gurukuls" where teacher and students live together and study. India has huge respect for their "Gurus" who are also called as teachers, philosophers, mentors. The ancient relation between teacher and student were co-cordial, personal and very close more like family member. The profession of a teacher was having a high code of conduct. The teacher has big responsibility for moulding a child into highly intellectual and skilled person in one or vivid area. The knowledge given was of different areas so that a person develops in a holistic manner and a big source of information for next generation. The teacher's dedication for the students in such a manner that they don't even charge any fee and devote their life for the sake of better development of their students.

They give their soul for the imparting of right knowledge to them. Similarly, the students also have high respect for their teachers. They were like god to them, and the relation was more on mutual basis and very strong. Dedication for cause, sincerity, long term perspective in mind, doing from the heart and respect of each other is the basis of such a beautiful foundation. The system saw a change after the coming of Britishers.

Britishers have their role in bringing modern Indian Education System where the emphasis was given majorly in English Language. The system followed in this era has changed the position of teachers. The system promoted the use of books as source of knowledge and information and the duty of teacher was to just follow the pattern. This pattern has restricted the quantity and quality of education system. The teachers were just doing their duty and deep involvement was mission. There was examination system also introduced in this era which has made students to mug up things and keeping mind's intelligence as unexplored one. The teachers were just a means to track that students are going in right direction or not. The enriched knowledge and capacity that teachers were having has not been explored in this time. The system has gained a more mechanistic form where things are more mentally decided, and less heart or feelings are used. The emotional connect between student teacher has gone down.

7.3. Transformation prerequisite in education system in India

The change in education system after coming of Britishers has taken education system at back foot. The education system needs to revamp in various aspects. The major once are the having open mindset, Away from rigidity, respect as Individual, Mindfulness and Heartfulness. Instead of focussing on quantity aspect this era demands the role of heart and quality in whatever capacity one can contribute. The mindset needs to be rebooted to make valuable contribution in education and in society as a whole. The era requires more respect for each other and feeling of positivity towards others. The scenario is aspiring for real synergy effect which can be done through heart-to-heart conversation and genuinely aspiring well-being of others.

Since the education system is the backbone of the society and the students of today will frame the future citizens, we need to set right example and shape them in best possible right way of heartful leadership. There are certain areas which need to be given focus, they are:

a. Quality vs quantity

This again must entail changes as over the last years, education system has started giving emphasis more on quantity rather than the quality aspect. The knowledge quality has been ignored at many places and the education industry has also been treated as business which completely dilutes the sanctity of education system in India.

b. Openness

Openness brings a clear picture of what the people feel and also the flaws of the system. Once people know the bottleneck, system can always set the things right. This requires the open environment which is free from any fear. The students when provided an open atmosphere in Institute, they can come up with the actual issues they are facing and so the solution can be worked out. This has to begin with open discussion among management and teachers and the things will then percolate down. The openness has to embrace heartfulness in that which will bring a humane touch and improved relations.

c. Consciousness

Empathy with involvement: Empathy is not only sufficient for heartful leadership but instead involvement with empathy is required. Teachers have big role to play in shaping life of a student and every student is different. Teacher has a responsibility to have a humane face and try to understand the problem of various students through empathy with an orientation of deep involvement. This creates a strong bond between teacher student relation.

d. Care

The heartful leadership has one more important component which is called as "care". A leader in today scenario requires to be caring for the team and for the people around. A caring attitude will help in understanding the other person situation and act accordingly. A humane touch for helping and understanding other creates an aura of positivity and gives strength to tackle the situation. Care of students to teachers, care to faculty to faculty and then student will also reciprocate the same care to other people in the system and in the society.

e. Courage

Courage is one thing that keep fear out and gives strength to fight with odd situation and pave way for brighter future. Courage throws away fear and there the space created for heartful behaviour. The emotions, the role of heart is there in each relation be it a student teacher, teacher-teacher, leader-teacher etc. The courage will further provoke the strength to speak truth and ask for fairness in the system. The courage has strong role to play in heartfulness. Even the two are interrelated in some aspect like a heartfulness will provide high courage to individual to face the challenges and survive.

f. Composure

There may be times when someone's point of view might be different, and person may lose temper very often. In order to prevent such situation, people have to be calm and compose. The composure attribute helps in handling difficult situation. This quality helps in giving time for the grasping things and then think from mind and heart together for paving out the right way. The behaviour shown impacts the behaviour of other and create an atmosphere of trust and belongingness.

Figure 10: Four Cs for heartfulness

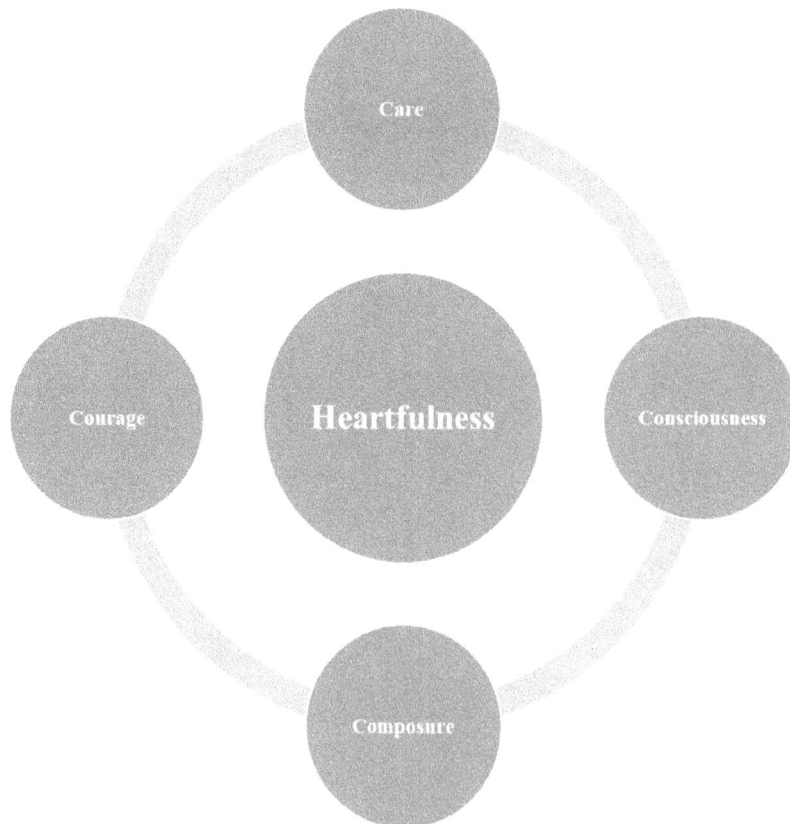

7.4. Impact of socio-economic change on sustainability

After LPG (Liberalisation, Privatisation, Globalisation) the country has gone a major change in various aspects. The change began at that time is still continuing at fast pace and gained momentum now. The current era is an era of change. Year 2020 has brought a revolutionary approach is all aspects of life. This year has seen lot of changes majorly due to impact of COVID-19. This Covid-19 has created a turbulence in vivid aspects majorly as Health, Hygiene, People Movement, Social Distancing, Business transformation and Technology as mode of contact and working. These all are the right set of examples of a VUCA world where the country demands more of Local Products to boost economic development. More than economic development, the time has made us understand the urge for humanistic approach for sustenance and growth. After churning of lot of discussion at various levels, there is realization of the need to connect people to each other emotionally. This will help to create own strength for not only facing the challenges but also to make a landmark and set example for others. Mental health is being given a lot of importance. In taking care of mental health, emotions need to handled well. Emotions when handled well, then the mental wellbeing is also appropriate. Person when think from mind along with the involvement of heart also, heartfulness approach comes into play which is upcoming requirement in current scenario. Heartfulness can be imbibe better when we include this in our education system. This will create a new generation who will understand the relevance of heartfulness and thereby will create an environment where the role of heart cannot be ignored we will land up in beautiful country where empathy , concern, care , humanistic approach will be in the blood of people.

Figure 11: Heartfulness and sustainability

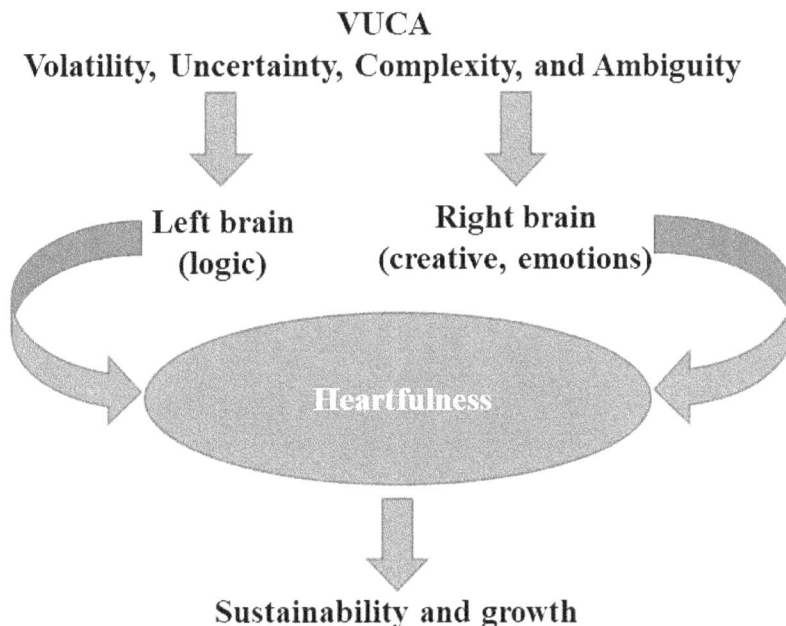

VUCA
Volatility, Uncertainty, Complexity, and Ambiguity

Left brain (logic)   **Right brain (creative, emotions)**

Heartfulness

Sustainability and growth

7.5. Conclusions on heartfulness and sustainability

The heartfulness approach in education system can help in creating totally different students where the focus is more on quality rather than quantity. The heartful leadership as a transformative process illustrated in the following figure will create a pool of students where their mental and physical wellbeing will be more appropriate to face the challenges of market and survive. Wellbeing promotes creativity and innovation in people which almost a mandate in corporate word to thrive and sustain. These all things promote a sort of synergy build in with various relations in personal and professional front which gives strength to flourish and bloom in fierce competition.

Figure 12: Emerging elements of heartfulness in leadership

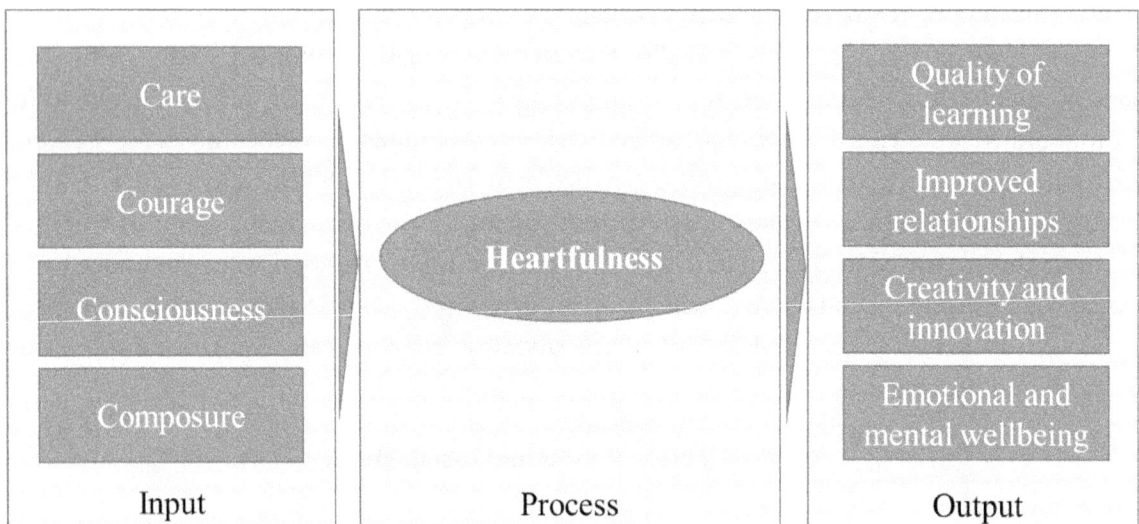

The heartfulness leadership in education system can modify behaviour in constructive way to create a sustainable environment. The step begins with self-transformation towards heartfulness and the contagious attribute of goodness will spear dots wings for a brighter and happy future.

References

- Kwee, G. (2015). Pristine mindfulness: Heartfulness and beyond. In E. Shonin, W. Van Gordon, William, & N. Singh (Eds.), Buddhist foundations of mindfulness (pp. 339-362). Springer

- Määttä, K., & Uusiautti, S. (2014). Love-based leadership at school as a way to well-being in pupils-theoretical and practical considerations. International Journal of Education, 6(3), 31-46.

- McCrea, N., & Ehrich, L. (1999). Changing leaders' educational hearts. Educational Management & Administration, 27(4), 431-440.

- Murphy-Shigematsu, S. (2018). From mindfulness to heartfulness: Transforming self and society with compassion. Berrett-Koehler.

- Uusiautti, S., & Määttä, K. (2013). Love-Based leadership in early childhood education. Journal of Education Culture and Society, 4(1), 109-120.

Chapter 8: Heartful leadership for a global social good - An action intervention in school education

Abhilasha Singh

8.1. Introduction

I distinctly remember the first chapter of the school management course I pursued while studying for the Bachelor of Education degree. The first chapter of the book opened with the following lines, "Eton is not known for its building. It is known because of its' Headmaster". It is many years later when I aspired to become a school leader and was mentored by Capt. Aj Singh – Headmaster and CEO/Director of Pinegrove School, Kasauli in Himachal Pradesh, India that I understood the true significance of how school leaders are drivers of change, leading school improvement effectively and creating champions in teachers and students alike. I also then understood how good leaders inspire leadership in others. I am a product of the same leadership mechanism. So let us look at school leadership in its entirety wherein I explore the Heart and Soul of Leadership. Following this I shall focus on how heartful education can be the catalyst for sustainable education.

It is believed, and much research has gone into, that 'Leadership from the Top', although required in some situations, is in fact unsustainable. I personally see myself as a leader, one that is at the center of influence and often ask myself, "What is impactful leadership?". Impactful leadership is visible in students through their achievements, enabled and supported via the empowerment of the teacher. For the same to happen the leaders must establish the school as a center of culture and learning for it is the school culture the reflects the ethos of the school and the heart of the curriculum the student's voice. The responsibility we have as leaders is to discover our own living 'breath' so that we can awaken and remind those we work with, of theirs.

8.2. Heartful leadership in education: My personal experiences

Successful leadership is about building a relationship, network and culture of the school. However, heartful leadership is when a leader connects the heart and soul of the institution and creates a vision to define it. It is an intelligent head and an intelligent mind that enables the leader as well as the individual to move forward and a heartful leader will help empower the team, guiding them forward through challenges while balancing the two intelligence. They empower the individuals with skills and gives them direction to pursue meaningful and purposeful actionable pathways.

Heartful (which is also heartful through empathy) Leadership must include some reference Spiritual Leadership. It is not about how we journey but rather where we journey and even more why do we journey. While the leaders should find answers to the above questions, they must also reflect on what their own vision for the institution is. This will enable them to find their own convictions of a meaningful life These are the thoughts that have guided my own leadership. I was fortunate enough to be placed as the Head of Section of Girls at the New Indian Model School (NIMS), Dubai in 2015. Preceding the same I have also held senior leadership roles in India and was Principal of a start-up school in the agriculture heartland of Haryana. I established a school for the children coming from agricultural families, uplifting them with the 21st century learning skills through various programs. I am grateful to God for that opportunity. However, it is with NIMS, Dubai that I realized my true potential and purpose as a leader. NIMS, Dubai gave me an opportunity to bring to my girls a leadership that empowers them to take part in intra-school Co-education events, something they were forbidden from earlier.

Keeping in line with the values and ethos of the school, I went ahead with a single-minded determination to introduce the girls to a rich learning experience. In 2016, a team of 10 girls stepped outside the threshold of the school to cross international borders and attended the Young Scientist program at NASA, USA. Establishing the school Model United Nations club was the next project. The girls were made to believe in the motto of "From the school MUN to the Real UN". This was accomplished with the school MUN team participating in WIMUN'2018 – the flagship event of WFUNA on the UN4MUN rules or procedure or the WIMUN Approach. Krishna Sateesh of Grade 9 was selected to deliver her position paper in the opening plenary at the UNGA, UNHQ, NYC. I still get goosebumps thinking of the accomplishment a 13-year-old achieved that day. Along with her, two delegates namely Shifana Sherin and Murshida Begum were selected as the Vice Presidents of their respective committees. The team made history and inspired the other girls in school to step out of their comfort zone and work hard to reach the stars. All of them now are accomplished young ladies having added many new feathers to their cap.

It is heartwarming to say that I live my dreams through my Children. Model UN is a simulation of the United Nations. It is a brilliant platform for students to develop 21st century competencies. It provides students with opportunities to discuss world problems and provide sustainable solutions for the same. In addition to skill development, it also helps the students to develop empathy and awareness about global sufferings, encouraging them to take action. It provides them with the space to reflect on the privileges they have and generates a sense of gratitude in each one of them. It brings humility to the students as they step into the shoes of a diplomat and negotiate to find innovative solutions to international problems. All of this cumulates into a very powerful experience.

UNESCO has identified 4 pillars of education supporting the notion of a life-long learner.

1. #LearningtoKnow: by combining broad general knowledge with the opportunity to work in depth on a small number of subjects. This also means learning to learn, to benefit from the opportunity's education provides throughout life. It's aims is to provide individuals with the cognitive tools required to better comprehend the world and its complexities, and an adequate foundation for future learning.

2. #Learningtobe: to develop one's personality and act with greater autonomy, judgement and personal responsibility. The aim is to provide individuals with the self-analytical and social skills to develop to their fullest potential. Accordingly, education must not disregard any aspect of a person's potential, including memory, reasoning, aesthetic sense, physical capacities and communication skills.

3. #Learningtodo: to acquire not only occupational skills but also, more broadly, the competence to deal with many situations and work in teams. It also means learning to do in the context of young people's various social and work experiences. These can be informal, as a result of the local or national context, or formal, involving courses, alternating study and work. This pillar aims to provide individuals with the skills to effectively participate in the global economy and society.

4. #Learningtolivetogether: by developing an understanding of other people and an appreciation of interdependence – carrying out joint projects and learning to manage conflicts – with respect for the values of pluralism, mutual understanding and peace. This exposes individuals to the values implicit within human rights, democratic principles, intercultural understanding and respect, and peace in society and human relationships. It enables individuals and societies to live harmoniously.

Lifelong learning is central to these four pillars of knowledge. When and what to teach should be complementary and interrelated in such a way that all people can get the most out of their specific educational environment throughout their lives. Unfortunately, many systems of education from around the world still emphasize the acquisition of knowledge over other types of learning. As promoted by UNESCO and many others, "a more holistic approach to education is needed" to enable each and every person to become a lifelong learner.

We cannot talk about education while neglecting its scope with the Sustainable Development Goals. On 25 September 2015, the UN General Assembly adopted the 2030 Agenda for Sustainable Development. This new global framework to redirect humanity towards a sustainable path was developed following the United Nations Conference on Sustainable Development (Rio+20) in Rio de Janeiro, Brazil in June 2012, in a three-year process involving UN Member States, national survey member states engaging millions of people and thousands of actors from all over the world. SDGs address a range of social needs including education, health, social protection, and job opportunities while tackling Climate Change and environmental protection as well as key systemic barriers to sustainable development such as inequality, unsustainable consumption patterns, weak institutional capacity, and environmental degradation. In order to reach the set goals, everyone needs to do their part: governments, the private sector, civil society, and individuals across the globe. A key feature of the 2030 Agenda for Sustainable Development is its universality and indivisibility. It addresses all countries – from the Global South to the Global North – as target countries.

By connecting the 4 pillars of Education by UNESCO to Education for Sustainable Development, it is clear that there is a wide chasm in education and equity and the way that education is delivered across the world. In the Indian context, the education system is marks-driven and focuses on teaching the textbook word for word. Year in and year out the schools move from one Academic year to another with a myopic view on education. At the end of the year the parents are largely merely bothered about the "marks" their children score on the Annual Report card and schools give in to that demand. Schools must provide a Holistic Education to their learners. A holistic approach to education believes that: Education is about educating the 'whole child'. Teachers must guide the student to become happy and well-rounded adults. We should teach students that they are interconnected with the world around them.

"Holistic education focuses on the fullest possible development of the person, encouraging individuals to become the very best or finest that they can be and enabling them to experience all they can from life and reach their goals[viii]

Dr. Jennifer Williams, founder of Teach SDGs and Co-Founder of Take Action Global, in her book Teach Boldly (2019) writes:

"With innovation and technology supporting us as we go, it is our time to lay out paths for people and the planet with our students[ix]".

Here is an example of heartful leadership. Being a passionate SDG Ambassador, amplifying my students' voices and empowering them with life skills has been my teaching and leadership mantra and motto. I remember one day when three little girls, Khadeeja, Sanya, and Salena, all in Grade 7, knocked on my office door and asked me if I had time for their idea. They were bothered about the exponential dereliction in the way plastic bottles were used in school and thrown. They were deeply concerned that our school was successfully contributing to the rise in percentage of plastics in the ocean. I smiled and told them I was listening. It was the germination of an idea that successfully went on to become the "Change Starts with You" initiative. The idea was to recycle single use disposable plastic bottles into artefacts.

They designed the Logo and presented it to the whole school during the morning assembly. I registered the project on Design for Change I Can program (www.dfcworld.com). The regulatory body KHDA, which directs private schools in Dubai, invited them for a presentation. Impressed with the idea, they invited the team to present their project during the Innovation Week celebrations. The project was selected by DFC amongst top three design thinking projects by schools.

8.3. Heartful leadership in education: Concluding thoughts

In my years as a teacher and the experiences that I brought to my senior leadership tenure, I have increasingly been mindful of listening to my students. I like to see myself as a commander during trench warfare, sitting down with my soldiers and getting my hands dirty. You cannot lead by giving directions from the atop. You have to sit with your team and ideate, build what you envision through your children. It warms my heart with pride to see my my Model UN team organizing the Inter School conferences with such ease, knowing that I did what needed to be done in order to enable that. I EMPOWERED my students with the right skills of leadership, enterprise, good communication and above all COURAGE and CONFIDENCE to go ahead and give the idea a try. Classrooms are an amazing place to initiate and engage in conversations with students on taking action to drive change. What is Social Good?

"Social good refers to services or products that promote human well-being on a large scale[x]." The idea of social good centres around three universal elements of: a. environment justice and sustainability; b. social inclusion; and c. peace harmony and collaboration[xi].

We, as leaders, have to ensure that we provide a spaces in school for engagement in actions centered around Campaigning, Advocacy and Activism. We help develop in our students the 21st century skills for strong communication along with skills in math, science and social studies. We must also build crucial competencies such as empathy, integrity, resilience and commitment to take action. Give back to the community in whatever capacity you can; Think Global and Act Local; Volunteer time of selfless service for the needy and the less privileged. These are my repeated submissions to my students.

A school is a sustainable machinery. It runs once the machinery is warmed up. Once the Academic year begins, it will end too. Syllabus will get over. But is that all that is there to schooling? We have to think beyond the pages of a report card. You have to see how enriching and colorful the school newsletter and Annual yearbook pages can be. We, in spite of knowing and believing that our work is towards building that final product – our students- with competencies to prepare them for the world they step into after school, year in and year out deliver content area lessons. I believe in developing the students' hearts and minds so that they can activate change, develop 'thinking' classrooms and, in addition to that, 'feeling' classrooms.

If we have never developed goosebumps whilst teaching, we have not experienced heartful teaching. I would like to mention my inspirations as becoming a Teach SDG Ambassador has been a very rich learning experience. It has brought the idea of global collaborations and much before we hit COVID 19 Lockdown and E learning in schools and higher educations, I was already facilitating SDG projects with educators from around the world with shared passion for Global Goals. This was my real work-life intervention as heartful educator and leader and this is what I practically believe the heartful leadership to be in context of education i.e. travelling extra mile for hope, smiles and development of future leaders of tomorrow!

Chapter 9: Empathy-driven interventions for fostering mathematical thinking among school learners.

Shalini Chauhan

9.1. Introduction

A kid comes home after school, throws his/her bag on the floor and declares to the parents "I'm not good at Math".

As a parent, there is a possibility that you must have witnessed this situation in your home. Probably you have heard a friend, a neighbour or a family member utter the same self-defeating statement. I always ask the following questions to myself, why do people not like mathematics? What would be the most important tasks for a math teacher in order to make learning math fun?

I believe in doing. I can read the eyes of my students. I can sense their feelings when they fail to answer the questions. I can also sense their desire to learning more with an unknown fear. I do not know if this is empathy or heartfulness but one thing I understand that the joy of seeing satisfied learner is beyond the expressions of the world. Through this case, I take the opportunity to share more about my practical interventions. Particularly, this case-based chapter focuses on helping teachers to know how to develop good and deep Mathematical knowledge among students.

9.2. The project of mathematics learning

Once I understood the quiddity of mathematics education, I started working on that and came up with these significant tasks that can keep math teaching easy and fun for the learners. How do you feel if your students start their class with positive self-talk about your teaching subject? The subject is not interesting or boring. It's a teacher who can make it interesting or boring. As a math teacher, I always want my students to have a positive attitude towards math and a deep understanding of mathematical skills. I know all parents have the same aspirations for their kids. Math is a basic skill, important to survive. This skill is necessary for all careers, from running a bakery to selling real estate. We use it every day e.g. planning for holidays, paying bills, shopping, monthly budgeting or saving for future.

More than just complete students I try to create complete people who can compete in the world with confidence. Have you ever believed in making your classrooms as interactive as possible and finding innovative ways to help students understand better other than just teaching from the book?

Being a teacher, have you ever thought about the most important fundamental concepts or conceptions in mathematical teaching? A teacher can set some tasks that can help to keep his/her teaching on the right track in achieving the goal.

Task 1: How and Why? Let us strive to teach for understanding the concepts and procedures of mathematics, the 'why' something works, and not only the 'how'. 'How' is procedural understanding. 'Why' is conceptual understanding. They both help each other in making learning easy and a fun. The teacher should have clear thought HOW and WHY the concept to be taught. Don't leave the topic until the learner both knows 'HOW' and 'WHY'.

This understanding does not come easily. It may take time. For example, Fraction is something a learner understands partially at first, and then deepen the concept over a few years. This is why many Math curricula are based on the spiral model.

In the spiral approach, topics are repeatedly addressed as learners move through the stages. The teacher does not assume that a learner has learnt and mastered a topic just because they have had an initial lesson on it. Instead, by returning to a topic after a period of time, the teacher builds in a review, consolidating the previous learning and adding in new skills and/or knowledge to enable progression. It helps in nurturing the learners' individual needs and focusses on experiential learning

Task 2: Work for the planning and goal: First of all, ask yourself the following questions. As for your teaching goals, are students really able to achieve them by the end of the course or are they too ambitious. Is there a logic to prevent course participants from merely studying for the test? Is there a link to real world problems and usefulness later in course participants' lives?

Our young learners should learn to handle money wisely. It involves good understanding in dealing with credit cards, budgeting and shopping. The goal should focus on preparing them for further studies in mathematics and enable them to understand information around them. Problem Solving, mental strategies and the ability to communicate ideas should be the integral parts of the curriculum.

Task 3: Let them learn to love math. One teacher can shape a child. One child can shape the world. First ask yourself: Do you like math? Do you love it? Why are you teaching this subject? Do you use math in your daily life? Are you passionate about it? Are you happy to teach math? This will show in how you teach it. A teacher cannot teach well if he/she doesn't understand or love the subject. One of the tasks should be let them observe the beauty of mathematics and to learn to love it. They should not feel negatively about mathematics. Try to create love for math. Teacher should be able to anticipate students' errors and should make them familiar with expected errors some of them are likely to make.

Task 4: Vary the instruction style. Some tips to create more interest among students for math or other subjects include the following. Think beyond textbooks to include riddles and puzzles. Start with a real-life challenge seemingly unrelated at first. Rely on example the course participants can relate to. Explore peer teaching or role plays. Ask them to design own experiments. Integrate latest technology such as online surveys building on competitions and rankings. Exemplify with powerful stories and manage the energies in the room. Always begin your topic with small introduction on why it matters, along with a short review of previous topic. Teacher should give short and simple instructions to make their understanding easy and fast. Ponder about questions-based teaching method, etc. The classroom layout should be in such a way that every learner should be approachable to the teacher.

Task 5: Know your way and tools. Teacher should have clear idea about the way of teaching and the tools he/she might use. A teacher must follow the concept of Active learning which means that learners take increasing responsibility for their learning, and we the teachers are enablers and activators of learning rather than lecturers or deliverers of ideas. Students should get actively engaged in learning and are approaching learning in a reflective and a thoughtful way rather than simply being the passive recipients of information that is given to them. How do you ensure learners are taking responsibility of their learning? Teacher should help the learners to build up the habit of reflection of their own learning, learning from their own mistakes, from experiences of other learners and this can be possible by a lot of sharing and collaboration in the classrooms. The learners should be encouraged not to hide from the discussion in the classroom. If you are able to spark the curiosity and interest among the learners, you can say that you are on the right path. The mathematical conundrums posed in the games helps a child becomes confident, innovative, reflective, engaged and responsible. In this way, a keen interest can be created among students to apply mathematical knowledge, and they can develop a holistic understanding of math. Ignite a love of learning with interactive tools and content that engage, motivate, and prepare each learner for success.

Task 6: Apply Confucian thinking based on the insight that I hear, I forget. I see, I remember. I do, I understand. There should be a method or a strategy to deliver your lesson which can make learning fun. Position the course clearly regarding established learning theories, such as Bloom's taxonomy. How might this be applied to learning about fractions in Mathematics?

Creating: Drawing diagrams to illustrate fractions - shading 3 squares out of 4.

Evaluating: Which fractions are bigger 2/3 or 3/5?

Analysing: Why is 2/3 bigger than 3/5? How do we know?

Applying: Practice putting fraction in order of size – equivalent fractions.

Understanding: Being able to use equivalent fraction to help carry out addition.

Remembering: Confident use of fractions in word problems and real-life situations.

Task 7: Making growth mindset statements. Learnings might look defeated when they say, "math makes me feel nervous" or "math makes me scared" or "I just can't do math". As a teacher, a facilitator and a mentor, there is a need to adopt a growth mindset – merely adding the word yet at the end of the sentence can change attitudes "we do not master math yet". Just try to create that spark among them so that they can change their self-defeating statements to self-motivating statements.

Mathematics may not be the most popular subject. Mostly, parents tend to dislike it, they find it difficult and communicate the same to their children that math is difficult. Then, learners also start feeling the same, especially when they don't get desired results in academics and it may cause phobia for math. There may be different reasons for this anxiety. Here, teacher as a facilitator can encourage them to reflect on how they understand mathematical concepts the best and also helps them to understand that although students learn in different ways, they all are equally effective as learners and can learn and implement the same concepts. They should understand and value their own learning style or approach. At the same time, they will learn to value their peers. Some learners are best in learning when they see, others are good at building things, some are creative but find it difficult to memorise formulae, some are good with words. There is a brilliant child locked inside every student. Try to improve a child's math skills by motivating him/her to learn in his/her best style of learning. I have tried a variety of methods in my classes.

9.3. Conclusions

We should aim to make our students mathematical thinkers not mathematical machines. Every child deserves a teacher that believes in them. Be that teacher! However, while doing this in my own class, I have learned that: first, work with the kids to understand their learning preferences and also their fear level; second, develop a plan which considered both group as well as individual special learning needs; third, work and engage with regular monitoring; fourth, keep the environment informal; fifth, make them feel that you are there to guide and not to punish. Remember, every student is different, but every heart is one!

Chapter 10: Ensuring that no one is left behind: Transparency and leadership challenges in education

Shabnam Siddiqui and Arya Dev

10.1 Introduction

The Sustainable Development Goals (SDGs) are a set of global ambitions agreed on by all United Nations (UN) Member States in 2015 as part of the UN's 2030 Agenda. These 17 goals guide national efforts to end poverty, reduce inequality, provide healthcare and education to all, tackle climate change, and much more. In sum, they should lead us to a better world!

Education is a human right and a force for sustainable development and peace. Every goal in the 2030 Agenda requires education to empower people with the knowledge, skills and values to live in dignity, build their lives and contribute to their societies. Ambitions for education are essentially captured in SDG 4 of the 2030 Agenda which aims to "ensure inclusive and equitable quality education and promote lifelong learning opportunities for all" by 2030.

As we as a country are still in search for solutions for sustainable development, good governance has always been recognized to be a critical tool for advancing sustainable development and a crucial element to be incorporated in sustainable development strategies. Good governance is also based on a conviction that a system placing sovereignty in the hands of people is more likely to invest in people, channelling public resources to basic education, health care and social services.

The 2030 Agenda clearly recognizes that the rule of law and development have a significant interrelation and are mutually reinforcing. As countries around the world are investing increasing efforts to live up with the expectations placed on them by the 2030 Agenda, the crucial importance of transparency and anti- corruption on sustainable development is appreciated more than ever.

10.2 Education: The bedrock for sustainable development

Good quality education is an essential tool for achieving a more sustainable world. To succeed in the race for Agenda 2030, policymakers must recognize that today's global imperatives – to eradicate poverty and improve wellbeing, while restoring the Earth's balance – form a single agenda, and that the most effective means of achieving it is education.

A strong education system broadens access to opportunities, improves health, and bolsters the resilience of communities – all while fuelling economic growth in a way that can reinforce and accelerate these processes. Moreover, education provides the skills people need to thrive in the new sustainable economy, working in areas such as renewable energy, smart agriculture, forest rehabilitation, the design of resource-efficient cities, and sound management of healthy ecosystems.

Perhaps most important, education can bring about a fundamental shift in how we think, act, and discharge our responsibilities toward one another and the planet. After all, while financial incentives, targeted policies, and technological innovation are needed to catalyze new ways of producing and consuming, they cannot reshape people's value systems so that they willingly uphold and advance the principles of sustainable development. Schools, however, can nurture a new generation of environmentally savvy citizens to support the transition to a prosperous and sustainable future.

The last 10 years have seen a global effort, led by UNESCO, to advance 'education for sustainable development', or ESD – a broad movement concerned with identifying and advancing the kinds of education, teaching and learning policy and practice that appear to be required if we are concerned about ensuring social, economic and ecological viability and well-being, now and into the long-term future.

Converse to the traditional way of teaching, Education for Sustainable Development means adopting a more holistic approach to education with the aim of 'creating a better world for this generation and future generations of all living things on planet Earth'. This allows every child to acquire the knowledge, skills, attitudes and values necessary to shape a sustainable future. Education for Sustainable Development is not only about being environmentally friendly; it also involves developing life-skills including leadership, communication and management; all of which are extremely important for personal development.

ESD aims to empower and equip current and future generations to meet their needs using a balanced and integrated approach to the economic, social and environmental dimensions of sustainable development. It incorporates key environmental challenges like climate change into core subjects like math, science and art, and involves modifying the teaching-learning process to a more all-encompassing approach. Students are thus able to relate what they learn in the classroom to their real life actions and will increasingly be in a better position to take the lead in changing behaviours and adopting sustainable lifestyles; the more this type of education is adopted.

A study[xii] conducted on the relationship between the sustainable development community and the education for sustainable development community states that the quality of the human and biospheric future depends on our collective capacity and ability to learn and change. Sustainable development is not itself sustainable (that is, lasting and secured), unless relevant learning among all stakeholders is central to the process. While sustainable development can be promoted through policy instruments, these tend to be effective for only as long as they are applied.

The logical corollary therefore is that unless stakeholders, policymakers, legislators, businesses, agencies, NGOs, the media and civil society are involved in learning processes, the proposed SDGs will not be achieved. Of course, we cannot secure a sustainable future in a matter of months. But, with a well-designed set of commitments and targets, we can move onto the right path. And, with effective educational programs that instil in future generations the importance of restoring Earth's balance and delivering a prosperous future for the many, rather than the few, we can stay on that path.

10.3. Good governance and transparency: Key to all locks of SDGs

While many factors play an important role in development, good governance is a critical tool for advancing sustainable development and is a crucial to be incorporated in development strategies. Good governance promotes accountability, transparency, efficiency and rule of law at all levels and allows efficient management of human, natural, economic and financial resources for equitable and sustainable development, guaranteeing civil society participation in decision-making processes.

For accomplishing the targets of the global goals, it is crucial that governments and stakeholders put in place transparent, participatory and accountable mechanisms to review the implementation of national and international progress from the onset. Transparency will also empower businesses to gather the necessary information about their supply chains, communication channels and risk management and assessment systems to implement changes and meet their sustainability goals. As a result, businesses can also make progress towards achieving the SDGs by the 2030 deadline.

No matter its approach and interpretation, there is an international consensus on the need to promote sound governance as a foundation for development. The challenge facing all societies is to strengthen institutions, processes and mechanisms that enable full participation of citizens in setting an agenda for sustainable development, which is also the essence of SDG 16. Upholding the rule of law in order to bring security and predictability to social, political and economic affairs is a cornerstone of good governance, beside the demand for accountability in public affairs, efforts to promote transparency and openness, decentralization and an increased role for civil society.

The SDGs aim to achieve economic, social and environmental sustainability by 2030. Corruption has the potential to undermine the successful implementation of all 17 goals. Without meaningful action against corruption, progress towards the other goals is likely to be extremely limited, hampering economic growth, increasing inequality and inhibiting prosperity.

Corruption thrives in conditions where accountability and institutions are weak, and where there is a shared expectation of corrupt behaviour. The collective and systemic character of corruption also makes it difficult to address. Corruption deeply undermines legitimacy and trust in public institutions and shapes people's perceptions of government performance and state effectiveness. It skews the distribution of public services and has a disproportionate impact on marginalized and vulnerable groups, leading to increased inequality. While many forms of corruption affect both men and women, it disproportionately affects women, who also represent a higher share of the world's poor.

This makes achieving the anti-corruption targets in SDG 16 more urgent than ever – not only because they are important for promoting transparency, accountability and integrity for their own sake, but also because they can serve as a baseline to achieve the successful implementation of all the remaining SDGs. Corruption is intrinsically linked to all 17 SDGs, going way beyond institutions and financial flows to affect services and sectors we deal with every day. Sometimes these issues hit closer to home than we might ever expect.

The principles of open government are embedded across numerous SDGs where transparency, public participation and accountable public institutions are instrumental to achieving a particular target. Under good governance, there are clear decision-making procedures at the level of public authorities and civil society participation in decision-making processes. People need relevant information in forms they can understand and use, as well as skills and motivation which facilitate change, through communication, education and new participatory mechanisms.

A study[xiii] clearly shows through case-studies that "weak legal and judicial systems – where laws are not enforced and noncompliance and corruption are the norm – undermine respect for the rule of law, engender environmental degradation, and undermine progress towards sustainable development." Emphasizing the correlation between lack of good governance and corruption the authors assert that – "The severe deficiencies in the rule of law encourage high rates of corruption which, furthermore, lead to a loss of confidence of economic actors. In turn, the role of investment decreases and slows economic growth, thus depriving governments of resources to invest in education, health, housing etc. and environmental management, all of which are "critical to sustainable development."

10.4. Inter-linkage between education and transparency

There are obvious flaws of corruption like disrespect of fundamental rights - as Corruption undermines democracy, governance and human rights by weakening state institutions that are the basis for fair and equitable societies with access to justice for all; and denial of basic services - as Corruption diverts funds intended for essential services such as health care, education, clean water, sanitation and housing. It represents a major hindrance to a Government's ability to meet the basic needs of its citizens.

Corruption hinders the achievement of SDG 4. Examples of corruption in education abound. Academic fraud, for instance, is widespread in many countries and considered a serious threat to integrity and reliability of certification in higher education. Procurement wastage in the education sector, including school buildings, false maintenance costs, "ghost" or absentee teachers featuring in the lists of active teachers, and textbooks paid for but never received, cost the public dearly. As a result, educational opportunities for the poor are limited in many parts of the world.

On the other hand, education is a crucial element in any attempt to effectively address the phenomenon of corruption. Through increased knowledge of the risks of corruption and its effects, it is possible to foster attitudes that do not tolerate corruption and develop skills that allow for individuals to resist social and cultural pressures when faced with corrupt practices.

With increasing awareness of the adverse effects of corruption on development, the strategy to counter it is now a top priority in policies around the world. One of the efforts to prevent corruption is by inculcating the young generation through education that has the character of anticorruption.

A considerable number of economists believe that corruption is likely to hamper education expansion and to reduce the ability of a country to form a high-quality human capital. United Nations Convention against Corruption (UNCAC) therefore requests States to undertake public education programmes, including school and university curricula.

Teaching materials Anti-Corruption Education is needed to foster anti-corruption culture in young generation especially with learning activities. It aims to create a culture of anti-corruption to students that Anti-Corruption.

Humans might not be born with integrity or the behaviours we associate with it, like honesty, honour, respect, authenticity, social responsibility, and the courage to stand up for what they believe is right. It is derived through a process of cultural socialization -- influences from all spheres of a child's life. In their school environments, students acquire these values and behaviours from adult role models and peers, and in particular, through an understanding of the principles of academic integrity. When students learn integrity in classroom settings, it helps them apply similar principles to other aspects of their lives.

With very serious thoughts going into sustainability issues globally, India has to make sincere attempts at devising policy and institutions in the education sector so that beginners are better equipped to make reasonable choices for a sustainable future. While girls' education has received some attention as a result of global advocacy and national schemes like Beti Bachao. Beti Padhao and Mid-day Meals, a wider view of education is needed and should undoubtedly include the street children and children with special needs together with children from economically weaker sections, Scheduled Castes (SC), Scheduled Tribes (ST), Other Backward Classes (OBC) and minorities. The motto of 'leaving no one behind' and overall inclusion in SDGs can truly be achieved only through transparency in all these schemes and missions.

The government is constantly making alterations and revisions and introducing new methods to enhance the overall educational sector of the country. Many initiatives have been undertaken in order to improve the quality of education right from the junior classes in schools. India's data-rich education system and open school data has effectively contributed to improving transparency and accountability. Recently, schools are being transformed by a series of developments in educational technology and these latest innovations has brought more transparency in the education system.

An application called 'Shagun' has been launched by the MHRD in August 2019 in order to increase transparency and accountability in the education system of the country. The digital platform will enable parents to send feedback as well. It will give vital information regarding the availability of schools nearby along with improved levels of transparency and accountability.

10.5 Conclusions on the role of heartful leadership in driving transparency

Corruption has major implications for expanding access to schooling and improving education quality[xiv]. There must be a change in the thinking process of citizens, students in particular through massive mobilization and enlightenment campaigns. This can be sustained through education.

The resilience of the youth "can do spirit" which have seen us through very trying times and moments must be brought to bear on the fight against corruption and sharp practices. Key institutions and agencies of national integrity like, the judiciary, police, vigilance organizations etc. must have the independence, strength and effectiveness to carry out their responsibility without hindrances. The empowerment of the people will enable them to effectively discharge their participatory role in governance, which is a sine qua non of a representative form of government in a republican democracy. Right to information, which can be ensued only through education, is necessary for openness and transparency.

We must adhere to the cliché of solemnly pledging to hold governments and industry to account for providing us a country that is corruption-free, transparent and accountable. Governments that provide basic services to its citizens and businesses that make transparency work for sustainable development.

However, institutionalizing the transparency requires leadership commitment at all levels in the organization. Under the current (conventional) framework of leadership development, the focus on ethics and transparency appears more theoretical than being pragmatic. The innovative approaches like 'heartfulness' can be a good point to restructure the leadership and management education framework which in turn would aim at creating multiplier effect through education, training and research related to heartful leadership for transparency and sustainability.

Chapter 11: Conclusions

Wolfgang Amann

Heartfulness as the core concept presented in this book should complement the recent international and increasingly popular debate on mindfulness. There are many reasons outlining the necessity to complement mindfulness. First, if we look at gross domestic products (GDP) across economies, the following pattern emerges. 50-60% of a developed economies' GDP are transaction costs based on inefficiencies and control efforts, leading to what Weibel (2017) labels "bullshit jobs" (p. 161). While markets might well become more efficient over time, lowering these transaction costs, their underlying foundation is a lack of trust. What if a generation of heartful leaders and managers create better organizations and behaviours? Valuable resources could be spent on innovation, equality and equity, or environmental upgrading and not degradation. Yet as of not, widespread distrust leads to even more opportunism as Weibel (2017) argues. There are limits to established economistic thinking, which needs to be replaced with a better paradigm. A balance-seeking, holistic refocusing on humanism in business and society should grant centre stage position to heartfulness. It can save and free hundreds of billions of Euros and enable different career paths.

This train of thought equally questions the dominant role mindfulness receives. James (2020) argues just how great a role model the late Steve Jobs must have been. Mindfulness can cause a neuroscientific change and alter the physical cingulate attention-ensuring cortex. James (2020) argues that this mindfulness can help concentrate better and for longer, stay calmer when in stress, boost creativity and become more efficient and effective. But for what? It is of course beneficial that more mindfulness can help us see the world through more and different lenses. It can foster self-acceptance, prevent or at least somewhat counter biases and prejudices, and revisit or rewrite old narratives. But what should we become more efficient and effective for? Mindfulness cannot be a value-free technique. It is incomplete if more efficient and effective individuals are not pairing their new skills with a moral compass. Authors in this book relied on Swiss pedagogy expert Pestalozzi (1746-1827) claiming that the educational ideal is the combination of cool head, warm heart and working hands. Mindfulness seems to overemphasize a cool head, also alerting that at times hands are too busy in today's hectic world. Following Pestalozzi, the cool, mindful head must be complementing with a warm heart, i.e. heartfulness. This can materialize with an orientation towards the United Nations Global Compact Sustainable Development Goals, national sustainability visions, an organizational sustainability strategy, or personal values. The concept of heartfulness presented in this book underlines the necessity to foster a warm heart in education and illustrated ways to conceptualize and operationalize this practically.

We do not live in normal times. COVID-19 has amplified the signs of unsustainability and reversed progress made when fighting poverty, inequality or inequity. We close this book when the world is still competing for receiving vaccines first and sufficient quantities. Geopolitical warfare still persists where some countries do not embrace but discredit scientific, medical progress made by rival nations. Multilateralism seems to have been suspended, giving way to a new wave of protectionism and nationalism in the fight against COVID-19 although the threat is a global one – unlikely to be solve by one country alone without multilateral coordination.

COVID-19 is not the only threat. While individual governments and companies struggle to keep their economies and operations going, artificial intelligence is accelerating its progress. Schleicher (2020) clarifies in this context that the future of learning cannot consist of what we have been doing and teaching over the last decades for long gone times. It is about smart pairing of what AI can take over and what humans with their innate creativity, emotions and lateral thinking can accomplish. Schleicher argues it is foolish to believe humans should try to and actually could catch up with what AI and corresponding software and hardware can do. Instead, we should focus on becoming first-class humans, not struggling to reach the status of second-class robots. More curiosity, compassion and courage can help add unique value without competing with AI. This aspiration requires a holistic revolution and not evolution of the education sector – with heartfulness at its core and heartful leadership at its upper echelon.

As authors and editors, we understand that it might well be quite a journey to design, mobilize for, direct, and sustainably implement this system-wide reorientation. Corresponding strategies have to be local and situational. They cannot merely come off the shelf in ready-made blueprints. Institutional leaders, however, have to not only show this heartfulness, which is very much in line with Pestalozzi's thinking. They, too, and not only the learners, have to excel at the tripartite challenge of cool head, warm head and working hands. If this book helped spread the call for this system-wide shift, if we inspired and encouraged positive change towards more heartfulness, then we have achieved our goal. We wish you as the reader all the best in your personal, situational endeavours!

References

- James, G. (2020). Neuroscientists confirm that Steve Jobs was decades ahead of his time. https://www.inc.com/geoffrey-james/neuroscientists-confirm-that-steve-jobs-was-decades-ahead-of-his-time.html

- Schleicher, A. (2020). Schooling first class humans. https://www.linkedin.com/posts/world-innovation-summit-for-education_learning-for-a-new-world-activity-6747109051936579584-gn1s/

- Weibel, A. (2017). Better safe than sorry. In B. Frey & D. Iselin (2017), Economic ideas you should forget. Springer.

About the authors

Dr. Pankaj Gupta is a Global Academic Leader with successful professional experience of over 25 years - as a Professor and Researcher, a Leader and an Institution Builder. Before joining as President, IIHMR University, he was associated with O.P. Jindal Global University (Delhi NCR) as Professor and Executive Director. He has earlier served in senior leadership positions in several top organizations worldwide such as IMT Ghaziabad, IIM Kozhikode, Symbiosis, the University of Washington among others. Dr. Gupta has an extensive network with various national and international universities and organizations and possesses several directors, board level positions in various organizations and corporations. Dr. Gupta has a strong understanding of higher education worldwide, especially management education and transformative leadership, creating innovative management eco-systems, identifying and recruiting the right talent, nurturing and retaining them and thus making a significant contribution to the organizations and the people. He is Ph.D., CMA, Fulbright Fellow (Washington), GCPCL (Harvard) and an alumnus of Lucknow University and IIM Ahmedabad. Dr. Gupta is the recipient of several prestigious awards including, the ' Fulbright Fellowship' by USIEF, 'Most Innovative Idea in Management Education Award' by IMC, ' Valuable Contribution to Profession Award' by ICAI, and 'Rashtriya Shiksha Gaurav Award' by CEGR, etc. Dr. Gupta has created an innovative model for 'Academic Audit' and 'Academic Quality Assurance System'. He teaches courses and gives consultation in 'finance & cost management' and 'self-awareness and mindful leadership'. Some of the organizations which have benefited from the training/consulting of Prof. Gupta include Maruti, Dabur, GE Capital, Ericsson, Electrolux, NTPC, LIC, Genpact, Bry Air, Samtel, Elin Electronics, Shriram Pistons, IREDA, NEC Corp, CBI, Indian Navy, etc. With numerous books, consulting projects and research papers to his credit, Dr. Gupta is a much sought-after speaker at top business schools, corporations, and organizations across the globe.

Prof. Dr.oec. DEdPsy D.Litt. (hon.) Wolfgang Amann graduated from the University of St. Gallen in Switzerland with a doctorate in international strategy. He is also a graduate of key faculty development programmes, such as Harvard University's Institute for Management and Leadership in Education, IESE Business School's International Faculty Program (IFP), the International Institute for Management Development's (IMD) International Teachers Program (ITP), the EFMD International Deans' Program and CEEMAN's International Management Teachers Academy (IMTA). Besides being active in top management consulting, he has designed and delivered executive education seminars and advised senior leaders for more than 20 years. He has published numerous books, articles and case studies. Previously, he was the executive academic director of the Goethe Business School, dean of Complexity Management, director of the MBA program family at the University of St.Gallen and project leader of the founding of the EBS University, a law school, a supply chain school and, most recently, CHEER – the Center for Humanistic Executive Education

Research at HEC Paris. He currently serves as professor of strategy and leadership, as well as the academic director of the degree, open enrolment and custom programs of HEC Paris in Qatar. He has received several research, teaching and impact awards as well as honorary professorships. Most notably, he won five CEMS best course awards.

Dr. Shiv K. Tripathi is Vice Chancellor at Atmiya University, India. India. Shiv leads Humanistic Management Network, India Chapter. Shiv has 24 years of experience in teaching research and education management. He is Formerly he was Professor and Dean at IIHMR University, Jaipur; Executive Director (Management) at Chandigarh University; Senior Professor and Dean at CMR University, Bangalore; Vice Chancellor at Mahatma Gandhi University, Meghalaya; and Professor and Head of Business Studies at Mzumbe University Dar Es Salaam Campus (Tanzania) and Dean, Faculty of Management at VBS Purvanchal University (India). His corporate experience includes advisory and board membership roles in different companies in India, South Africa and Tanzania including 3year advisory term at University of Stellenbosch Executive Education Limited, South Africa. He has published more than 75 articles, book-chapters and case-studies including six books on 'Management Education' and 'Executive Education' theme. He is member in United Nations Principles for Responsible Management Education (PRME) Global Working Group on 'Anti-Corruption in Management Curricula' and 'Poverty Eradication through Management Education.' Shiv has academic interest in ethics, humanism, sustainability, strategy, supply-chains, management education and higher education management.

Dr. Ernst von Kimakowitz is passionate about strengthening the positive impact of business and education towards a more equitable and more sustainable planet. He holds a research position at the University of Lucerne in Switzerland, is founding director of the Humanistic Management Center and co-founder of the Humanistic Management Network. Ernst held visiting faculty positions in Colombia, Germany, India, and Japan, is lead editor of the Humanism in Business book series at Palgrave Macmillan Publishers and provides training and advisory services on topics related to leadership, sustainability and business ethics.

Dr. Anand K. Joshi, is Advisor, International Skill Development Corporation, London. Formerly, Dr. Joshi has served as founder Pro-Chancellor of Atmiya University, Rajkot (India) and Founder Vice Chancellor of CMR University (India). During 35 years of his career in education management, Dr. Joshi has served on key leadership positions with national level regulatory bodies like All India Council for Technical Education, National Council for Teachers' Education and Indira Gandhi National Open University, India.

Prof. Dr. Umesh Mukhi belongs to Faculty of Management Department at FGV EAESP, São Paulo School of Business Administration. He completed his bachelors in Electronics and Telecommunication Engineering from University of Mumbai, India. He then moved to France where he obtained his Master's in management at Audencia Business School and his Doctorate in

Management from University of Nantes. He approaches the field of Management from transversal perspective and is passionate about pedagogical innovation for creating enhanced learning experience. His teaching and research interests encompass topics such as Role of Business Schools, Organizational Behavior, Sustainability, Spirituality and Cross-Cultural Leadership development. He has been visiting researcher at United Nations Principles of Responsible Management Education, New York. Umesh has also coordinated Master Program and Executive Euro MBA at Audencia Business School. He has also delivered training sessions for business schools, public and social sector organizations in Europe, Asia and Latin America.

Saurabh Saha is a Technology Leader with 18 years of experience in product engineering, product management, strategy and innovation across three geographies. He has also started 3 startups and made one exit. He is a Stanford Ignite Fellow, an iSpirt PNGrowth Fellow and more recently a Stanford's Code In Place Fellow. He won the hottest entrepreneur award in 2015 and was also featured by Economic Times. His chapter on education was published by Harvard University in a book on Nicola Tesla.He also ran a think tank for UNESCO Sorbonne's Club on sustainability. He has also been a mentor to several startups and is currently a mentor with IIM Lucknow. Over the last 3 years he has focused on the growth part of late stage startups. His last project was with an NGO in UP East as the Chief Operating Officer of the project, where he helped create 20 micro enterprises in one of the poorest regions of the country.

Dr Deepti Sharma is Associate Professor, HR at IIHMR University. She has rich blend of 13 years of experience in corporate and academics including her experience in Axis Bank , HR Professional in corporate and academics includes reputed institutes like Manipal University Jaipur. She has earned her Phd from University of Rajasthan in Employee engagement. She has Proven capabilities in working with cross-functional teams for evolving strategic vision and driving the overall operations. She has successfully organised and participated various Management programmes including HR Conclave, Conference, Seminar, workshop and FDP. She Participated in terms of Paper presentation in various national and International Conferences including Meiji University (Tokyo), Malaysia International University (Malaysia) etc. She also has research papers published in national and international Journals in various areas like Glass ceiling, Employee Engagement (EE), Employee experience (EX), Demonetization, Sentiment Analysis etc. Her area of interest includes Human Resource Management, Organisation Behaviour and Human Resource Planning.

Abhilasha Singh is Principal in an Indian Curriculum school in UAE. She has a vast amount of experience working with range of students including EAL, SEND and G&T students. She was awarded the Global Teachers Accreditation by British Council in 2013. Ms. Singh is also an international Model UN Trainer and a Teach Sustainable Development Ambassador cohort-3 2019 selected by Teach SDG Academy which partners with the UN to spread awareness about the Global Goals. She represents Dubai as an Ambassador for SDG's for Children, an international organization working to achieve Global Goals initiating projects with school students. A TEDx and GESS Speaker, she is a national level Handball and Basketball player. Teaching about Sustainable Development Goals is very close to her heart and she consider Global Goals – Agenda2030 to be a collective responsibility of all individuals. She was selected as a Facilitator by the Global Classrooms Goals Project for the month of Sept 2019 to guide 17 teachers from around the world to initiate project related to Sustainable Development Goal allocated to the respective schools.

Shalini Chauhan is a Mathematics Educator and Examination Officer at Indirapuram Public School, Indirapuram. Shalini is passionate about learning and has always tried to expand her knowledge by pushing the limits. Being in a field of education she finds it as an opportunity to live her passion. Since her early career years, Shalini was sure about her love for teaching, which was often displayed in her constant efforts in making peers understand difficult concepts. Since very beginning she has taken teaching as a passion and believes it's her duty to grow pro rata the journey of her students so that she can provide them with contemporary knowledge; and help build a better future of the world by making students better citizens. With over two decades of experience in school education, Shalini has deep passion about brining action interventions for sustainability impact of education. She holds Masters' degree in Economics and has also qualified CTET (Central Teacher Eligibility test). She is an active member of NGOs 'Nirbhed Foundation' and TIES. (Teaching and working for SDGs 4 & 5). Shalini is also SDG Choupal Advocate, T4 Ambassador, MIE (Microsoft Innovative Educator), Flip grid Certified Educator and Wakelet Community Member and Leader. Shalini is enthusiastic about helping the underprivileged in the society, and in this regard has undertaken the responsibility of teaching many indigent children for no fees. She has deep passion about brining action interventions for sustainability impact of education. She has written articles for different platforms, such as Cambridge TOT community and HigherTeacherEd.

Shabnam Siddiqui is Director at Centre of Excellence for Ethics, Governance and Transparency at United Nations Global Compact Network India. An academic practitioner with twenty-three years of experience, Shabnam specialises in developing and executing strategic interventions through multi-stakeholder networks, training and research and has several national and international publications to her credit. Shabnam is a great believer and practitioner of Collective Action, and believes that the private sector plays a critical role in the attainment of SDGs. Academically, she has a Masters in Sociology from India, a second Master in International Peace Studies from USA and embarked on a PhD in Public Policy at Singapore. Her most recent foray in academics was as a Chevening Rolls Royce Innovation, Science, Policy and Leadership (CRISP) Fellow at Said Business School, University of Oxford. Shabnam is an amateur wildlife photographer, and intends to work towards the holistic development of forests and wildlife.

Arul Dev is Programme Analyst (Legal) at Global Compact Network India. A law graduate from Faculty of Law, University of Delhi, he has appeared before the Hon'ble Supreme Court of India, the Delhi High Court and the Patna High Court. He is a legal and governance professional with over 8 years of cross- sectoral experience in Litigation, Legal research, CSR, Sustainable Development and

Governance issues. Though having a considerable legal experience in areas of litigation and other juridical matters, he has fervently pursued legal research, policy advocacy and stakeholder strategizing. He specializes in synthesizing research, drafting and content writing. He is a strong advocate of a principled approach to sustainable and socially responsible corporate policies. From being a legal professional to a sustainable development practitioner, his heart lies in action-oriented governance and building networks for community development. He is an avid reader and a film aficionado.

Endnotes

---

[i] Cf. https://heartfulmethod.com/ for details.

[ii] Cf. https://heartfulness.org/webinar/pearl-webinar-archive/heartful-leadership-a-new-look-at-leadership/ for details.

[iii] Cf. https://indiacsr.in/ubuntu-humanism-and-heartfulness-necessary-for-responsible-leadership-in-healthcare-sector/

[iv] Cf. https://www.youtube.com/watch?v=aY7m6oYr8Ww

[v] Cf. Source: www3.weforum.org/docs/WEF_Future_of_Jobs_2018.pdf

[vi] Cf. https://hbr.org/2005/10/the-office-of-strategy-management

[vii] Cf. https://www.denisonconsulting.com/knowledge_center/

[viii] Cf. https://helpfulprofessor.com/holistic-education/ accessed 07/18/2020

[ix] Cf. https://www.goodreads.com/book/show/45834474-teach-boldly accessed 07/13/2020

[x] Cf. https://journals.sagepub.com/doi/abs/10.1177/1049731518793271?journalCode=rswa accessed 07/15/2020 (p. 762).

[xi] Ibid.

[xii] Cf. https://doi.org/10.1177%2F0973408214548360

[xiii] Cf. https://docplayer.net/12514465-Rule-of-law-good-governance-and-sustainable-development.html

[xiv] Cf. https://www.econjournals.com/index.php/ijefi/article/viewFile/781/pdf

www.ingramcontent.com/pod-product-compliance
Lightning Source LLC
Chambersburg PA
CBHW081403270326
41930CB00015B/3396